# DAY CARE FOR INFANTS

# DAY CARE
*FOR* # INFANTS

*The Case for Infant Day Care
and a Practical Guide*

*By* E. BELLE EVANS
*and* GEORGE E. SAIA

*Beacon Press    Boston*

*This book is dedicated to the children of the Castle Square Day Care Center.*

# CONTENTS

## ACKNOWLEDGMENTS

We should like to acknowledge Robert Evora, Supervising Manager of the Boston WIN team, whose faith and support of our preschool teacher training program have enabled many welfare parents to gain economic independence and provide a better standard of living for their families.

We extend special thanks to the teachers at Castle Square whose dedication to children has demonstrated that high-quality infant day care can be achieved.

The authors are particularly grateful to Elmer A. Evans for his constructive criticism and his painstaking editing of the manuscript. We also wish to extend special thanks to Clara E. Evans for the many long hours she spent typing various drafts before the final manuscript was finished.

Finally, we hope that our efforts may aid all who are aware that quality day care is one of the most pressing needs of our modern industrial society.

INTRODUCTION

Day-care services for children three to five years old are rapidly being established in most communities, but some people still question the desirability of day care centers for infants (children under the age of three). Providing group care for children under three remains an area virtually untouched, as evidenced by the lack of available literature on the subject. The few studies comparing the development of infants in child-care settings with those reared exclusively in conventional family environments have shown no significant developmental differences between the two groups. Nevertheless, until these findings became known, researchers assumed that infant care would produce the same deprivation effects found among institutionalized children. Data showing the tremendously retarding effects of institutionalized care have often been applied erroneously to day-care settings without regard to differences in both structure and services. Unfortunately, such outdated attitudes are held by many professionals to this day.

The impetus for this book derives from the authors' desire to ensure the development of optimum day-care provisions for infants. In defining "infant day care" we mean any place where children under the age of three years are cared for in groups by warm, understanding, responsible adults. Many infants at home, when visiting or playing with neighborhood children under the supervision of their mothers, might fall within this category at various times throughout the day. However, for purposes of this book, we shall limit our discussion of infant day care to those places specifically established to care for young children in groups outside their homes.

Only quality infant group care will be discussed, since we feel that custodial care or mere baby-sitting arrangements are inadequate not only for our own infant but for any infant. Moreover, we believe the development of infant day-care services for children under three is a logical next step in the evolution of child-care practices in America's industrial society. This change, however, should not be regarded as detrimental. On the contrary, the development of infant day care should be seen as an excellent opportunity to create new patterns of child care to meet the needs of an ever changing American society. From the outset it should be understood that we are not advocating that all children be placed in day care centers, but we do believe several alternatives should be available to parents for care of their children.

Much can be learned from other countries which have pioneered in early-childhood group care; many have had well-established child-care services for a long time. In most of these countries day care is financed at least partially through government subsidies. Comprehensive quality child-care centers have been provided with expert consultants in various fields. The components of such programs include medical, nutritional, psychological, educational, and social services. Bruno Bettleheim and Urie Bronfenbrenner have recently described patterns of child rearing in Israel and Russia, respectively. (See Appendix: Relevant Readings.) They have demonstrated that children under three may be reared effectively in day care centers if essential ingredients of child care are provided.

Recently we returned from a tour of five Western European countries, Yugoslavia, and Russia. The purpose was to observe the operation of infant centers and to discuss with child-care directors the various components of their programs. The information we acquired was instrumental in developing the infant-care unit at the Castle Square Day Care Center in Boston, Massachusetts.

The Castle Square Center began in 1969 as a storefront nursery school for twenty children, three to five years old. It was located within the Castle Square Housing Project. Because of the tremendous need for day-care services in this area, and the encouragement and support of the Division of Family Health Services, Massachusetts Department of Public Health, the original nursery school program was extended to a full day care center. Two additional classrooms were opened for a two-year-old group and another family group consisting of three- to five-year-olds.

It soon became apparent that many mothers in the community needed child-care services for children under two. In addition, many of the teachers in training and the staff at the center also required care for their infants. Thus the center responded to the needs of the community for infant day care, and the program was expanded to the present census of 130 children, 72 under the age of three. Even with this increased capacity for infant care, there are long waiting lists for every infant classroom, indicating the tremendous need for direct-care services in this area.

Because we knew the high standards of program operation established at the center, and we had seen how well other children were developing, we were convinced that there could be no better environment in which our own child could grow. When Evan was one month old, we placed him in the infant class at Castle Square, and Belle returned to work full-time as director of the day care center.

Through our experiences as parents with an infant in day care, as well as through our expertise in developing and operating an infant day care center, we hope to make this book helpful to the reader. Whether you are interested in establishing an infant day care center of your own, in expanding an existing child care center to include infants, in attempting to choose an infant center for your child, or whether you are a mother at home interested in learning more about how you might be able to stimulate your child's development, this book should provide some helpful suggestions.

The first section will deal with the whys of infant day care. Included will be a discussion of the various theories of child development related to such child-care patterns and relevant research findings for both this and several other countries. The models selected present widely diverse examples of group infant care. Evaluation of such existing models can aid in the development of quality infant day care in the United States.

Part One is designed to survey the present concern regarding the care of infants and put it in proper perspective. It does not pretend to be a complete theoretical analysis of such care facilities.

Part Two is a practical guide to help you develop an infant day care center. Included are a brief survey of the rules and regulations required for licensing infant day care centers; suggestions on writing proposals, devising budgets, and securing funds; how to select appropriate personnel to work with very young children; finding and developing a site to provide a suitable environment in which infants may develop; and, finally, the content of a program to encourage optimal physical, emotional, intellectual, social, and psychological development in very young children.

*Painting Christmas decorations (Evan at seven months)*
*Castle Square Infant Center*

*Use of feeding tables*
*Castle Square Infant Center*

*Dramatic play in housekeeping area*
*Castle Square Toddler Class*

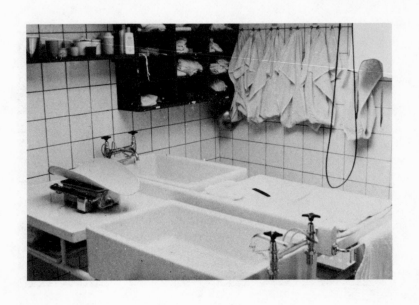

*Change area*
*Infant Center, Sweden*

*Elevated laundry area with carpeted steps*
*Castle Square Infant Center*

*Use of platforms and tubes for climbing*
*Castle Square Toddler Classroom*

*Use of carpeted and tiled play area*
*Castle Square Infant Center*

*Large and small muscle toys*
*Infant Center, Sweden*

# PART ONE

# The Case for Infant Day Care

CHAPTER ONE

# Day Care for Infants?

"You're going to place your baby in a day care center!" How many times we were greeted with this incredulous exclamation. We were able to live on one income, and yet we wanted to put Evan, our one-month-old baby in day care. Why? No one seemed to understand, even when we explained our reasons.

First, we had noticed that babies in the Castle Square Infant Center always had someone to play with and something to do. We recalled how Belle's homebound girl friends would put their babies in a playpen or crib while they went about their household chores. Even though the baby would often protest loudly against isolation, the housework had to be done, and this seemed the most efficient way to handle the situation.

In contrast, at the day care center teachers had no other responsibilities to distract them from their primary involvement with the infants. They were free to "play" with the babies all day, stimulating infant learning and providing a warm, child-centered environment.

Moreover, we were impressed with the effects "multiple mothering" had on the infants in the center. Since the staff ratio for children under age three is one adult for every four children, and teachers work staggered shifts to cover the ten-hour day, each infant is exposed to at least four or five adults in his classroom. From early infancy he must learn to relate on more than a one-to-one basis.

What is the effect of such care? The infants at the center are outgoing, friendly, curious babies who expect and receive warmth and comfort from adults. We believe this helps them envision their world as a worthwhile place, filled with adults who are interested in helping them learn and grow.

These positive experiences with multiple mothering are not unique. Studies of multiple mothering in day care have demonstrated no detrimental effects on either the emotional or the intellectual development of the children. In fact, before the advent of the nuclear family, most children were exposed to the influence of sisters, unmarried aunts, and grandmothers. Day care in this sense replaces a socializing influence lost in the last two generations. Research has shown that various mothering practices produce differing patterns of socialization, but do not result in the deprivation effects observed in the institutionalized child of the hospital or orphanage. The reason is, we believe, that parents remain the primary caretakers of their children; day-care teachers merely supplement this care.

"But your child won't even know you!" Ridiculous. This is absolutely not true. All children in the day care center know their mothers and fathers and greet them usually with an excited, open-armed welcome. At four months, Evan responded with a smile to our voices, and waved his arms in an excited greeting whenever we came to play with him or to take him home.

Even infants reared at home are exposed to a variety of different contacts, such as relatives and baby-sitters, and parents normally do share child-rearing responsibilities with others. When a child is in day care eight to ten hours a day, parents still retain the primary role for socialization, since the principal attachment of the child is to the parents, and the child has a permanent position within the family.

Studies confirm these observations at the day care center, and demonstrate that the quality (personal involvement) of the mother-child relationship rather than the quantity (mother at home, but minimally involved) makes the difference. For example, in one recent finding, American mothers ranked second only to English mothers (around the world) in the *least overall time spent with their children,* even though most American mothers remain at home.

Besides the fear of diminishing the mother-child bond, some people still view day care as a form of institutionalization which will produce the devastating results documented by many researchers in the past. This concern is dispelled by recognizing that day care and institutionalization are not the same. Day care is only part-time care, whereas institutional care is full-time. Day care is a supplement to the home, whereas an institution is a replacement for the home. Furthermore, staffing within day-care settings provides a stable adult-child relationship, while institutions provide an ever changing rotation of adult caretakers. Thus, in orientation, purpose, and quality of care, day care and institutions are different.

Another concern at this time stems from new discoveries that enormous strides in growth and development may take place in the early months of life, that it is possible to enhance cognitive and emotional development in the very young child. For the past several decades, psychologists have attempted to isolate types of learning in order to study them in depth. The principle of classical conditioning through stimulus-response was demonstrated by Pavlov in his experiments with dogs. Operant conditioning, through the use of rewards and/or punishments, was studied by Skinner and has been employed by mothers and teachers for centuries.

Most recently there has been tremendous interest in cognitive theory—the process of thinking, reasoning, and problem-solving. The Swiss psychologist Jean Piaget has done extensive studies of the development of children's logic. He classified into categories various concepts of the physical world (time, number, space, and so forth) held by children at different ages. Piaget believes children learn through active participation in their environment and attempts to find causal explanations for events are essentially an adaptation necessary for survival as thinking human beings.

It should be obvious to even a casual reader that encouraging early learning for children through educational programs and toys is clearly "in vogue," especially in middle-class America, as many parents attempt to provide intellectually stimulating experiences for their children. It seems that today's parents are far more concerned about their young children's intellectual competence than parents in the past. Recent studies have heightened this interest by dramatic demonstrations of increased IQ scores when children are exposed to stimulating environments.

In the scramble for gadgets, toys, and gimmicks which promise to increase abilities, the key element producing competence in children may be overlooked. A recent study begun in 1965 at Harvard University under the direction of psychologist Burton White has documented information on competency development. The researchers have discovered a critical period in infancy—that eight-month period between the tenth and eighteenth month of life—during which the pattern for intellectual competence is set for life.

Fortunately, Dr. White and his associates do not just make this pronouncement. Instead they methodically describe specific intellectual and social skills which competent children possess by age three and that other children lack. In addition, they compare the characteristics possessed by mothers of competent children with mothers who have failed to produce such skills in their children.

Dr. White believes that it is the attitude of the child's primary caretaker (usually his mother) that holds the key to the important difference between children in the area of competence. He states that competent children have mothers who are effective both directly, as consultants to their children, and indirectly, as organizers, designers, and rulers in their child's physical environment.

Who are these mothers of competent children? Surprisingly enough (or not so strange if one really thinks about it), mothers of competent children are often working mothers who do not spend a great deal of their time interacting with or "teaching" their children. Dr. White estimates that these mothers give their children less than one or two hours a day of undivided attention, or about 10 percent of a child's waking time. Evidently the amount of time spent with a child is far less significant (according to this and other studies) than is the quality of the mother-child relationship.

What then are the elements that comprise this vital quality situation? Through painstaking tabulations, Dr. White and his researchers discovered that the dominant activity of a one-year-old child is looking at his environment—studying, staring, and gaining information. One-fifth of a toddler's waking hours is spent in this fashion. A rich physical environment, well stocked with interesting and exciting objects for the toddler to examine, is of the utmost importance.

Just looking, however, is not enough. In order to develop competence, a child must touch, taste, bang, and otherwise experiment with a rich assortment of toys and household objects. In addition, toddlers must be free to roam safely throughout their environment while exploring and learning. Devices which restrict exploration such as gates, playpens, and high chairs, when used for long periods of time, thwart a child's curiosity and may even stunt his intellectual development.

Are we supposed to redesign our homes to fit the special needs of the developing toddler? Many other people, adults and children alike, live together at home, and even if such a re-designed household were better for one toddler, why should the other individuals who live in it be inconvenienced? Clearly, no one would want to live in a home designed exclusively for a tod-dler, except perhaps another toddler.

What then is the solution? A compromise can be reached in the home whereby dangerous objects and poisonous solutions can be locked away from reach and breakable objects stored away while the toddler is exploring and does not understand re-strictions.

Another, less disruptive, solution is to have a special center designed for children where they are free to explore without disrupting the lives of other family members. Such a physical environment can be produced readily in a day-care setting.

That early childhood holds such a pivotal position in an individual's life is at once a reason for hope, but also for pos-sible despair if nothing is accomplished during these early form-ative years. Studies of children from deprived backgrounds indi-cate that such children begin school at a severe disadvantage. A vigorous national effort to tackle the problems of the poor was launched during the 1960s. In 1966 alone, Congress allotted over a billion dollars for the War on Poverty.

One of the most exciting programs developed in the last decade was Operation Head Start, a nationwide preschool edu-cation program for disadvantaged children. Follow-up studies indicate that in order to begin to assist children reared in pov-erty, programs must begin before age five and last for several years longer than the one year originally assigned to the Head Start classroom. The Pre-Kindergarten program now enrolls children at age three, and follow-through programs have been developed to provide former kindergarten Head Start· children with a Head Start type program for first, second, and third grades.

These programs have stimulated interest in early learning. Day care will help demonstrate the positive effects of high-quality group care for the very young child. Such programs as Pre-Kindergarten, Head Start, and Follow-Through are child-centered in orientation. They attempt to improve the child's concept of self by providing activities in which he can learn, and experience a sense of accomplishment and pride. Theories in child development stress the importance of such an orientation for the well-being of the child.

Research in child psychology has demonstrated the importance of the early years, not only for learning but also for total personality integration. The psychoanalytic theories of Freud and Erikson traced deviant behavior in adults back to its source in early childhood.

Learning or behavior theory stresses the importance of the preschool years also. Since the most important aspects of behavior are learned, early learning experiences play a critical role in the child's development throughout life. Using this knowledge, day care can set the stage on which these new learning experiences may develop.

A final fear regarding day care is that it will make all children too much alike, stifling individuality. Nothing could be further from the truth. While it is true that there are times when most children do the same thing at the same time (meals, naps, field trips), most of the time children in a child-oriented center are involved in activities they choose themselves. Mothers at home cannot afford this child-centered luxury, since usually infants must accompany them on adult errands.

Moreover, in a one-to-one situation, the mother's values, wishes, needs, desires, and expectations are readily imposed on the developing child, who often becomes a symbiotic extension of the mother through whom she attempts to fulfill her own unrealized ambitions. This is destructive to the mother, since she herself does not develop a true image as a person, and it is especially destructive to the child who often must live out his mother's unfulfilled dreams rather than realize his own identity.

Children may enjoy a better chance of developing their own individuality in a child-care center where the personal emotional investment of many adults is dissipated rather than in a highly intense one-to-one mother-child relationship in the home.

We have found that children raised in groups at the day care center are highly individualistic. In fact, promoting individual development is one of the major goals stressed at the

Castle Square day care center. Mothers are pleased with the development of their children in day care. The children seem to learn quickly from other children in the group. Information about the infant center and the quality of care children receive there has produced long waiting lists for the three infant classrooms.

The need for infant day care is tremendous. Almost half of all American mothers work, and of these, two out of every five have children of preschool age. It is estimated that by 1980 there will be 5.3 million working mothers with ever increasing day-care needs for their preschool children.

In the past, day-care services were thought to be necessary only for the underprivileged and families which had no means of support except the mother's income. Thus day-care services were seen only as a temporary placement, and as soon as possible mothers should return to the home and remain with their children. Today this attitude is changing.

Recent statistics from the Women's Bureau of the U.S. Department of Labor show that less than one-half ( 43 percent) of working mothers are from poor families (incomes under $6,000). Fifty-seven percent of working mothers, therefore, have a family income of over $6,000, and of these, 48 percent lie within the middle-income range ( $6,000 to $10,000). One out of every five working mothers comes from a family where the combined income is more than $10,000. These figures clearly demonstrate that many women are now working for reasons other than financial need.

The emerging thrust for child-care centers is coming from additional segments of the population. Women's Liberation groups are demanding that a choice be given to women between remaining at home with their children or having children cared for by others for part of the day. Many women resent being told how to raise their children by individuals who are often least involved with providing direct child care—mainly male researchers and middle-aged and/or childless women professionals.

Recently the federal government provided preschool Head Start experience for two million children, some as young as three years old. The present provisions of the 1967 Social Security Act call for a network of day care centers to be established across America to receive children of women on welfare, with the aim of enhancing the employment opportunities of the mothers. To date, however, no money has been allocated for such a system. It remains to be seen whether the American people are willing to pay the cost of ensuring that their most precious natural resource—children—be given the best-quality care possible. We feel that all children, not just the poor, are due this right to quality care as citizens of the wealthiest nation in the world, whether care is provided children exclusively in the home, or supplemented by day care.

Why are infant-care services not available, even though so many mothers need and want them? One reason is that researchers assumed infant care would produce the same deprivation effects found among institutionalized children. Data showing the tremendously retarding consequences of institutionalized rearing have often been applied erroneously to day-care settings, without regard to differences in both structure and services. To this day such outdated attitudes are still expressed by many professionals. For example, one expert in child development has stated that the best day care can be is "mildly malevolent." More recent studies comparing the development of infants in child-care settings with those reared exclusively in conventional family environments have shown no significant developmental differences between the two groups.

Another roadblock to infant day care has been a male-chauvinist attitude, casting women automatically in roles solely as mothers and wives, forcing them to follow in the footsteps of their mothers and grandmothers. After World War II the "domestication" of the American female was favored by Dr. Benjamin Spock. He idealized the exclusive role of motherhood for women and proclaimed that the very lifeblood of America, i.e., the children, was entrusted to them. Under Spock's leadership, the American mother took charge of developing the latent individual potentialities in each of her children. This task was to consume her waking hours, as she strove to mold each child, in the meantime sacrificing her own self-fulfillment and identity.

Such examples of male chauvinism are prevalent even to this day, as noted in the recent informative book by Dr. T. Berry Brazelton, *Infants and Mothers:*

An understanding of the importance of their role as mothers, as well as a realization of its potential in their families, may help them (women) see it as a goal that transcends anything they can achieve in their professional life. This is a goal for the future education of women.

Also:

> It [motherhood] is likely to be the most demanding challenge a woman faces except that of no longer being a mother . . .

We disagree completely with this educational recommendation for women, since we believe it is the epitome of male chauvinism. Such concepts, although reinforced through the nuclear family, have come under serious scrutiny by many people today, especially the young. Young women are questioning the role of the housewife in our present society; many feel that role is not to their advantage. Such reservations are not without foundation. Studies indicate that women who have remained at home in the sole role of mother and housewife have a far more difficult period of menopause than women busy with careers not associated directly with childbearing or rearing. Some housewives, aware that their role in life is disappearing as their children grow up and move away, find renewed purpose by having a "caboose" child, consciously or unconsciously assuring a need for them as mother for an additional fifteen or twenty years. Indications are that caboose children find difficulties in peer relationships, since they are reared according to the standards of a bygone era.

A final obstacle to quality infant day care is the enormous expense. Because of the need for an intense adult-child relationship, quality supervision, and responsible child care, a minimum ratio of one adult for every four infants is recommended. In order to assure quality personnel, adequate salaries must be paid. The cost of the service becomes extremely high. Quality care for a child under age three costs a minimum of $56 per week per child at the Castle Square Day Care Center. Children aged three to five years cost $40 per week per child.

Taking all these factors into consideration, it should be readily apparent why infant day care has had a very slow start in the United States. In spite of the fact that such care is desperately needed by many women, and wanted by still more, it remains almost unavailable for legal, social, and economic reasons.

However, do not become discouraged. The problems are difficult but not impossible to solve. As Robert Kennedy once said: "The difficult can be done immediately, the impossible takes a little longer." We have written this book to try to help you make the seemingly impossible less difficult.

In summary, we believe that quality infant day care is not only a valuable supplement to exclusive home care, but in fact may be an improvement over typical home care because it stimulates an infant's physical, emotional, social, and intellectual development.

No home could possibly contain all the toys, games, and large-muscle-building equipment found in a well-equipped day care center. Children develop coordination and control as they run, jump, skip, hop, and climb under the watchful supervision of adult caretakers. Both indoor and outdoor play provides children with opportunities to develop large-muscle skills.

Smaller, manipulative materials such as puzzles, beads, and blocks assist in the development of fine motor coordination. In a quality day care center, children are not pressured to accomplish tasks beyond their abilities. Instead, they are surrounded by a rich environment—and sympathetic adults who encourage and assist them to develop both physical skills and a positive concept of self. Such a concept emerges from the successful mastery of meaningful skills.

Infants' emotional development is facilitated in day care when they are exposed to various ways of ordering their behavior and dealing with their feelings. Understanding teachers who have a basic knowledge of child development can help children learn to handle such emotions as anger, fear, jealousy, and friendship in a constructive manner, thus promoting emotional growth and development.

In addition, a child in quality group day care is exposed to a diversity of both peers and adults. He learns to interact with each, and develops important social skills such as sharing and cooperating with others.

Finally, intellectual development is promoted in a day-care environment which encourages children to examine, explore, and discover. Language skills are enhanced as children talk with each other and with adults. Pictures are explained, and storybooks read to individual children or to children in groups, and all youngsters are encouraged to respond to a variety of stimuli. Field trips to places outside the home and classroom setting stimulate curiosity and help to promote intellectual development. When such trips are reinforced by classroom activities, true learning takes place.

We are convinced that a quality infant day care center does enrich the lives of very young children and promotes physical, emotional, social, and intellectual development. Our answer to the question "Day Care for Infants?" is an emphatic Yes!

## CHAPTER TWO

# Infant Day Care Abroad

Recently we visited infant day care centers in four European countries—France, Denmark, Sweden, and Yugoslavia. We obtained data through interviews with day-care personnel and by on-site observations. We were able to get firsthand information about the operation of child-care centers in these countries, including a description of the environment, child-care programs, staffing procedures (qualifications and patterns), training, and delivery of associated services.

Although we traveled throughout western Russia and spoke to several day-care personnel, we were unable to visit operating centers due to a cholera epidemic at that time. To supplement our own meager experiences in Russia, we have included accounts from other authors. And we have added a brief description of child-rearing practices within the kibbutzim of Israel.

### RUSSIA

*Description*
Infant group care is not a new phenomenon in the Soviet Union. The idea of rearing children in groups originated far back in Soviet history. Since 1956, however, the Twentieth Party Congress has called for expansion of existing nurseries and kindergartens, and has also created two new types of schools: *internats* (boarding schools) and "schools of the prolonged day." The major difference between these two forms of child care is that at boarding schools children return home only for special occasions, whereas at schools of the prolonged day, children return home each evening at 6:00 P.M. The educational curriculum is essentially the same at both schools.

At present only 5 percent of all Soviet children over the age of seven attend one of the newly created schools. Nursery schools, however, enroll over 10 percent of all children.

The apparent aim of all Soviet child-care institutions is to supplement home care from infancy onward in order to provide the psychological, social, and physical environment necessary for optimal development. There is some question whether or not the family is subordinate to the schools, or vice versa. Since such a close relationship exists between home and school, the primacy of either is difficult to substantiate.

### Program

Two major features stressed in Soviet *yoshi* or "crèche-kindergartens" (two months to seven years) are collective living and programmed stimulation. An example illustrating the promotion of collective living is the infant communal, or group playpens. Six to eight infants are placed in such areas at a time. Face-to-face interaction is promoted through raising the playpens to the eye level of "upbringers" (nurses).

As children mature, group games are introduced, and toys designed for collective play are provided. In a Soviet kindergarten, children are not encouraged to play alone since this might develop individualism. As children grow older, the upbringers withdraw from the direct leadership role, and the children begin to monitor and discipline each other. Monitoring, encouraging, and assisting others are qualities encouraged in order to implement collective living. It is hoped that through early socializing experiences children will become both self-sufficient and at the same time considerate of others.

Programmed stimulation is initiated early. Nurses are well trained in stimulation techniques and sensory motor functioning. Specific times during the day are allotted for such activities.

All Soviet children are placed on a daily schedule at the crèche. Doctors work with nurses in developing these schedules for eating, sleeping, and stimulation. Whenever possible, children of a particular age level will be placed on the same schedule.

Infants are swaddled in warm clothing and placed out of doors for a portion of each day. This practice of conditioning the child to his environment is very common in Northern European countries. Physical activities in the outdoors for older children are compulsory.

### Group Size and Adult-Child Ratio

Depending upon their location within factories or industries, or association with collective farms, and the numbers of children involved, day-care schools are designed to accommodate groups of approximately 90, 140, or 280 children. Children under the age of three attend a *yasli*, while the older children go to a *detshy sad*. Within the *yasli*, babies are divided into the following age groupings: infants aged two to six months, six to nine months, and nine or ten months to one year; toddlers from one to two years old; and children from two to three years old.

In good centers the babies are cared for in groups of seven or eight by a nurse and her assistant *(nyanya)*. Thus a ratio of one adult to four children is maintained. However, in poorer centers group size increases to twelve to fifteen babies under the care of three upbringers, a ratio of one adult to six or seven babies. Toddlers are cared for in groups of fourteen to sixteen by two upbringers, a ratio of one adult to seven or eight children.

### Staff

Directors of institutions are trained in pedagogic colleges. In America this would be comparable to three years of undergraduate study. Upbringers are also trained in the same institutions. Their education consists mainly of on-the-job training under constant supervision and evaluation. Because of the lack of personnel in this area, older women *(babushkas)* often help with the care of babies. This practice, however, presents problems; despite supervision the *babushkas* often revert to traditional methods of child-rearing, which sometimes conflict with the new state policies.

### Hours of Operation

The number of hours a child spends in day care depends upon the kind of center he attends. In boarding schools the child comes home only on special occasions. At the *yasli* children usually arrive between seven and nine in the morning and leave between four and seven at night. In addition to weekdays, some centers remain open Saturday mornings. Overnight and

drop-in care can usually be arranged, since most centers attempt
to be flexible to respond to parental needs.

### Cost
In Russia the state assumes 75 to 80 percent of the cost for
day care. Parents pay on a sliding scale, usually between three
and twelve rubles ($3 to $12) a month.

### Associated Services
In addition to the director and upbringers, most centers
have a music specialist as part of their educational staff. A doctor is in charge of the medical component, and he/she may work
full time at the center if size warrants it. In addition to pre-
ventative measures (examinations, immunizations, and prophylactic measures of sanitation) the doctor refers children in need
of special treatment to the polyclinic or local hospital. A medical nurse and her assistant (if the center is large enough) are
responsible for not only the daily inspection of all children but
also for overall health supervision.

Soviet day care provides excellent nutrition. Older children
receive up to three balanced meals a day plus snacks. Babies
are placed on feeding schedules which the mother must follow
on weekends when the infant is at home.

In addition to educational, medical, and nutritional services, other associated services are provided as needed.

### Summary
There has been much interest recently in the Russian experience with day care. It appears that the Soviets are in the
process of modifying a rather rigid state-controlled educational
system. Although children are valued highly in Russia, and are
cared for with much love and affection by adults, they are regarded primarily as valuable resources in the rebuilding of the
new Soviet society.


### ISRAEL

### Description
The kibbutz is a child-oriented society where very little is
denied children. While aspects of the program vary, according
to the individual kibbutz, all phases of the child's development

—physical, psychological, social—are viewed by every kibbutz as the responsibility of its educational system. Not only do the children belong to their individual families, but they are also children of the entire kibbutz society. Since each member is responsible for both his family and all other members, all members take an interest in all the children.

### Program
Many infants join the nursery group within a few days following birth. Sixteen children who may range in age from four days to one year are cared for in the Infant House by a head nurse *(metappelet)* and her two assistants. The infant remains at the nursery, but his mother visits him often during the first six weeks when she is excused from work. If she is nursing, the mother returns to work only part-time and spends much of the rest of her day feeding, bathing, and dressing her infant. Fathers visit whenever they can.

When the child is six months old, he is allowed to leave the nursery for short visits to his parents' room. During his first year of life an infant interacts with his parents, nurses, and other infants.

When they are approximately one year old, infants are moved in groups of eight from the nursery to the Toddlers' House *(betpeutot)*. Here they learn how to feed and dress themselves, and become toilet trained. They are taught organized games and activities, but are also encouraged to participate in spontaneous play. Parents usually pick up their toddlers after work, around four or five o'clock, and spend the early part of the evening with them. In most kibbutzim, children eat with other children in their own dining hall and return to the Toddlers' House to be bathed and put to bed by their nurse. However, in some kibbutzim, parents put their own children to bed. Such daily contact with parents promotes strong emotional bonds. However, it is primarily the child's nurse and teachers who guide him toward the collective goals.

### Group Size and Adult-Child Ratio
Most Infant Houses contain a maximum of sixteen children under the age of one year, and three nurses (one head nurse and two assistants), a ratio of one adult to 5-plus children. In the Toddler House children are cared for in groups of eight by two

nurses, a ratio of one adult to 4 children. Many kibbutzim have a nursery teacher (*gannenet*) to replace one of the nurses caring for the children when they reach the age of two or three. Between the ages of four and five, two former toddler groups of children are combined to form a kindergarten unit of sixteen children, now called a *kevutza*. One nurse and a kindergarten teacher care for this group of children, who remain together as a unit ( a ratio of one adult to 8 children) until high school.

### Staff

Most child nurses caring for preschool children in the kibbutz are not professionally trained nurses. Instead they are women from the kibbutz who like children and enjoy working with them. These women are given a training course in the care and rearing of young children, and are usually encouraged to take additional courses. Usually nurses care for the physical and emotional needs of children, while the specially trained nursery and kindergarten teachers handle the children's social and intellectual development.

### Hours of Operation

Infants remain in the infant house or nursery on a twenty-four-hour basis for the first six months of life. After that, children are allowed short visits with their parents (usually no more than two hours on weekdays) and return to their group house at night.

### Cost

All costs for the care and rearing of children are borne by the kibbutz.

### Associated Services

As members of the kibbutz, all children are given medical and dental care, and other associated services as needed.

### Summary

While there are varying accounts as to the success of kibbutz rearing of children, one fact does seem clear. Children can be reared in groups by other than their parents as long as the quality of care is good. The kibbutz children display none of the disastrous effects noted among institutionalized children, even though they remain apart from their parents for most of their lives. It appears that as long as children's needs are fulfilled by sensitive, caring people they will develop normally.


## FRANCE

### Description

Day-care services have been available to children in Paris for over fifty years. Because of the high living costs in Paris, usually both parents work. For this reason competition for available space is fierce, and pressure for expanded facilities enormous.

The administration of district day care centers falls into three categories: Departmental, run by the P.M.I. (*La Protection Maternelle et Infantile en France*), a branch of the general public assistance administration operating most of the day care centers in Paris; Municipal, run directly by local authorities; and Private, run by charitable, religious, or secular organizations.

Each crèche is a self-contained unit with classrooms, kitchen, laundry, office, storage, and outdoor space.

Before an infant is admitted to the group, he is undressed by his mother and then placed on a potty by the nursing assistant. Although there have been attempts to curb such premature practices, many infants as young as three months are conditioned on this regime. After "potty," children are bathed and dressed in school clothing. Only then may they join the rest of the children in the group.

### Group Size and Adult-Child Ratio

In the departmental day care centers are sixty children between two months and three years of age. Crèches are generally housed in separate buildings and children of different ages are grouped as follows: twelve *enfants* from two months to eight months; twelve *bébés,* eight months to eighteen months; twenty *moyans,* eighteen months to two years; and twenty *grads,* two to three years.

For the twelve *enfants* and twelve *bébés* there are four assistant child nurses (auxiliary *puericulturists*) per group, a ratio of one adult to six infants. In the two older groups of twenty children each, there is one child nurse per group, and an additional nurse who assists each group, a ratio of one and one-half adults to twenty children.

### Staff
The child nurses are called auxiliary *puericulturists,* girls who have taken a two-year vocational training program for assistant child nurses. Each center is directed by a graduate nurse, who has had an additional year of post graduate training at *L'Ecole de Puericulture.*

### Hours of Operation
Centers are open from 7:00 A.M. to 7:00 P.M., six days a week, with staff staggering shifts to arrange coverage.

### Cost
The cost is determined by a sliding scale based on parents' income ranging from 1.80 francs to 54 francs per week ($4.50 to $13.50). The French government gives an allotment to working mothers (2.3 percent of their salaries) to help offset this expense whenever the authorities deem it necessary.

### Associated Services
Associated services are especially well developed. Emphasis is placed on nutrition, with staff spending almost 50 percent of their time involved in functions pertaining to feeding or food preparation.

Young infants receive six bottles of formula a day, prepared in the formula kitchen by one of the child nurse assistants. Older infants are on a five-meal regime, consisting of milk and soft foods. The oldest children eat four meals a day—breakfast, mid-morning snack, lunch, and afternoon snack.

There is an isolation room for children who become ill during the day. A physician visits each center twice a week to give immunizations and routine physical examinations. He/she also takes emergency calls and makes additional visits if there is an epidemic or other illness. The physician is responsible for prescribing the diet of the youngest infants.

Social, dental, and psychological services are available under the state system of socialized medicine.

Children are brought to the main "consultation" center in

groups of twenty for yearly dental examinations, and treatment as necessary.

### Summary

While day care provided in France, and especially in Paris, is extensive and most comprehensive, we feel that excessive emphasis on physical care and hygiene interferes with learning and development. For example, children are not allowed to crawl on the floor or be placed in common playpens for fear of infection. In addition, there are too few adults to give adequate stimulation to the children.

## YUGOSLAVIA

### Description

The child-care system in Yugoslavia is organized in large collective units. Each center provides comprehensive care services for children two months to seven years of age, and drop-in services for school-age children seven to eleven years old whenever necessary.

Child-care centers are large (several hundred children) and divided into three major programs. The crèches care for children two months to three years of age; preschool classes, for children three to seven years of age; and drop-in centers, for children seven to eleven years of age.

The number enrolled depends on the size and needs of the community. In Zagreb, a large industrial city in northern Yugoslavia, total enrollment is 530 children in one child-care center.

There is a nonteaching director and a nonteaching educational supervisor, in addition to numerous nurses, preschool teachers, cooks, laundresses, and maids. A large commercial kitchen and laundry room, classrooms, storage area, and office space complete the center.

### Program

In the crèche at Djecji-Centar, Zagreb, there are 125 children between two months and three years of age. These infants and toddlers are housed on the second floor of an old building. Cribs line the perimeter of the rooms; toys are scanty; and available play area is limited. Infants remain many hours of the day in cribs, with little stimulation from their overworked attendants, who are kept busy diapering and feeding such a large group of children with similar needs.

### Group Size and Adult-Child Ratio

Children are grouped according to chronological age. The 125 children at the Djecji-Centar in Zagreb under the age of three years are cared for in groups of 25 by one nurse and one preschool teacher. Three hundred preschool children ranging in age from three to seven years are grouped as follows: three- to four-year-olds are taught in groups of 15 to 20 with one preschool teacher; four- to five-year-old children, in groups of 20 to 25 with one teacher; and children five to six years of age in groups of 25 to 30 with one preschool teacher.

### Staff

A preschool teacher is in charge of each classroom. These teachers have completed four years of secondary school plus two years of college. In the crèches, a child-care nurse assists the teacher. Child-care nurses have completed three years of secondary professional school.

### Hours of Operation

Child-care centers are open from 5:00 A.M. to 6:00 P.M. to cover parents' work schedules.

### Cost

The cost of child care is $30 per month, with parents paying on a sliding-scale basis, supplemented with local tax funds as necessary.

### Associated Services

Associated services are exceptionally well developed. Each center has a well-equipped commercial kitchen and staff. A breakfast of milk, rolls, and butter is served at 8:00 A.M., followed by a fruit or chocolate snack at 9:30 A.M. Lunch consists of soup, vegetables, salad, and meat, and there is an afternoon snack of cocoa or milk, bread and butter.

Each center has an isolation room for children who become ill during the day. A school physician visits the crèche three times a week to examine infants and toddlers. For children over three years of age he/she is available for emergencies. All older children are given yearly physical examinations. In addition to giving children periodic examinations and immunizations, the school physician is responsible for the inspection and maintenance of sanitary and health conditions.

Dental examinations are scheduled yearly through contractual arrangement between the center and a dentist.

An additional contractual arrangement with the state welfare agency covers all social cases as necessary.

Psychologists from the Department of Education make periodic visits to test all preschool children. Preventive suggestions are given to teachers, and children with special problems are referred to the Department of Mental Health for follow-up services.

### Summary

Because both men and women are encouraged to work in Yugoslavia, day care centers are extensive, and nearly all preschool children are enrolled in some care arrangement outside the family. While Yugoslavia provides extensive day-care services, we feel the quality of care and creativity of individual expression are diminished because of the state-dictated curriculum, large class size, and the high ratio of children to adults.

### DENMARK

### Description

In Denmark the day-care nursery system has been in operation for eighty years. Children between the ages of three months and three years are cared for in special houses called *Vuggestue*. Each is a self-contained unit consisting of classrooms, kitchen, and laundry. Both outdoor play areas and indoor office space are provided. The needs of the community determine the number of children enrolled. Although the *Vuggestue* may vary in size from about thirty to sixty children, the average center cares for approximately forty-two children.

Each center is staffed by a nonteaching director, one "head educator," and several assistant teachers for each classroom. Children's ages and the size of the group determine the number.

Supplementary services include a cleaning maid, a cook, and a laundress.

### Group Size and Adult-Child Ratio

Groups vary in accordance with the following classifications: A group of sixteen infants may consist of eight children from three to twelve months and eight children from twelve to twenty-four months, with a ratio of one adult to four children. A typical classroom unit for sixteen infants contains two bathing rooms (also used for diaper changing), two toilet rooms, a sleeping porch, an outdoor play area, and a divided indoor classroom area.

Older children, aged two to three years, are organized in groups of twelve to sixteen, maintaining the ratio of one adult to four children.

### Staff

The head teacher presides in each classroom. All head teachers have completed a special college program for preschool teachers. Their training program consists of the following:

3 months: College Classes (Child Growth and Development, Child Psychology, Educational Curriculum, etc.)
6 months: Apprenticeship Nursery School
6 months: Hospital Pediatric Aide
3 months: College Classes
6 months: "Au Pair"—Home Care of Children
6 months: Apprenticeship Kindergarten Class
3 months: College Classes
Comprehensive Examination

### Hours of Operation

*Vuggestue* centers are open from 7:00 A.M. to 5:00 P.M. To maintain adequate coverage the staff must work staggered shifts.

### Cost

The cost of care is 270 kroner ($36) per week. Parents pay 30 percent of the cost, and the balance is derived from state and local taxes.

*Associated Services*

Associated services are highly developed. Each center has a well-equipped kitchen, where the cook prepares all meals for the children and staff. A breakfast of porridge, milk, and vitamins is provided at 8:00 A.M.; a morning snack of milk or juice at 10:30 A.M.; a lunch of egg, fish, or meat, vegetable, pudding at noon; and a snack of teething bread, fruit, or milk in the afternoon. The menus are posted weekly, so parents will know what their children are eating.

Each center has an isolation room for children who become ill during the day. A doctor visits each center once a month and refers all problems in need of treatment to the child's own doctor. He/she examines all infants under one year of age every three months, and toddlers twelve to thirty-six months twice a year and in addition, gives all immunizations to children at the various child centers in his/her district.

The doctor is also responsible for referrals to other services, such as dental, social, and psychological agencies.

*Summary*

Since child-care centers in Denmark are viewed as social and educational institutions, theoretically all children are able to attend. In practice, however, many more parents wish to have children enrolled than space permits; hence an admission selection procedure is required, with preference accorded in the following order:

1. Single parent
2. Both parents students, or working, or a combination of both
3. One parent working, one parent at home

However, if mothers feel the needs for day-care services in their community are not being met adequately, they can petition for additional care centers.

The quality of child care in Denmark is excellent. The staff is adequately trained, and there are good adult-child ratios. Equipment and environmental needs are satisfactory, and the children appear to be both healthy and happy.

## SWEDEN

### Description

Child-care services have been available in Sweden for many years in *barnstuga*, centers specially built for children in day care. Each *barnstuga* is a self-sufficient unit, containing classrooms, kitchen, laundry, outdoor play, and office space.

Each *barnstuga* has about sixty children, ranging in age from six months to seven years. At least one *barnstuga* is built when any new apartment complex is constructed. Since new apartments are usually built as part of a "new town," all associated services (schools, stores, clinics, and so forth) are also developed at the same time. Because each new town is a self-contained unit, each *barnstuga* can draw directly on the comprehensive services available in each community.

Every *barnstuga* has a nonteaching director, a professional teaching staff, a cook, a laundress, and a cleaning maid.

All classrooms open directly onto large outdoor play areas surrounding the *barnstuga*.

### Group Size and Adult-Child Ratio

Children are grouped in accordance with the following classifications. In a group of twelve six- to twenty-four-month-old infants, there are three child-care nurses, a ratio of one adult to four children; in a group of twelve two- to three-year-old children, there are two child-care nurses and one primary school teacher, a ratio of one adult to four children; in a group of eighteen four- to five-year-olds, one child-care nurse and two primary school teachers, a ratio of one adult to six children. The oldest group, the five- to seven-year-olds, have three primary school teachers for eighteen children, a ratio of one to six.

### Staff

There are two classifications for teachers who work with children in the *barnstuga;* child-care nurses and primary school teachers. The child-care nurses have taken a six- to eight-month training program, preparing them to care for very young children. Primary school teachers attend college for two years, then serve a four-year internship before they are allowed to teach.

### Hours of Operation

The *barnstuga* is open from 6:30 A.M. to 6:30 P.M., with staff members working staggered shifts to arrange for ample coverage.

### Cost

The cost of care ranges from 15 to 100 kroner ($3 to $25) per week, with parents paying on a sliding scale based on family income, and supplemented by local tax funds.

### Associated Services

Associated services are highly developed. Each center has a well-equipped formula kitchen, in addition to a large commercial kitchen for food preparation. The cook prepares all meals for the children and staff. A breakfast of eggs is served at 8:00 A.M. At 11:30 A.M. the main meal is served, consisting of meat, potatoes, and vegetables. There is a snack in midafternoon, and a supper of sandwiches and fruit at 5:30 P.M.

Each center has an isolation room for children who become ill during the day. A doctor visits each center every two weeks, and refers children to their family physician for treatment whenever necessary. Immunizations are given at the *barnstuga* by the visiting physician. In addition, he/she refers all social and psychological problems to appropriate agencies as they occur.

From their third year, children in the *barnstuga* are given yearly dental examinations. In addition, all children at the *barnstuga* use fluoride toothpaste when brushing their teeth.

### Summary

While all children are theoretically able to attend the *barnstuga*, in practice the demand for child care exceeds supply. The following selection criteria have been adopted:

In order of preference:
1. Single mother who is working
2. Single mother who is a student
3. Mother and male companion living with child when one is working and the other is a student
4. Mother and male companion living with child when both are students
5. Mother and male companion who are both working

The *barnstuga* preferential criterion is matriarchal, based on mother's status and income. Husbands and unmarried male companions are classified similarly.

Of all the countries we were able to visit, we felt the day-care system in Sweden was by far the most comprehensive and best in quality. Associated services were well coordinated with the child-care centers. Staff members were well educated, and maintained excellent adult-child ratios. Equipment and environmental needs were superior, always appropriate to the age level of children served.

## CONCLUSION

The day care centers we have discussed reflect the fundamental philosophies of each country. Each system has been developed by its respective country to satisfy its own needs; yet as we look at them, the various day-care systems seem to fall naturally into three categories: Totalitarian (Russia and Israel), Authoritarian (France and Yugoslavia), and Democratic (Denmark and Sweden).

In Russia, because the labor of all is considered essential, and since the Communists wish to build a new social order, children are valued highly as precious natural resources to be developed and utilized by the state. In Israel the kibbutz has adopted a similar philosophy regarding the value of children, stressing loyalty to the smaller community kibbutz rather than the larger more impersonal state.

Since France has one of the oldest day-care systems, it seems to illustrate a traditional, authoritarian approach in delivery of day-care services. In our opinion, Yugoslavia has developed a compromise between the French and Russian systems of day care, reflecting its pivotal position in East-West relationships. Francophile by tradition, yet on the fringe of Western European influence, Yugoslavia is both a Slavic and a Communist nation; hence it is not surprising that it has attempted to meld the two philosophies within its day-care system.

As one should expect from countries evolving from a common Scandinavian heritage, Denmark and Sweden have similar day-care systems. To us their day care centers seem to encourage individual development far more than any other systems we have encountered and described. In our opinion, individual development to the limit of ability is the essence of the democratic way of life.

We do not recommend that you try to copy any one of these day-care systems in its entirety. You should examine each system carefully and take from it those ideas which seem to best fit the needs of your children and the wishes of their parents. Only by developing your own composite day care center can you meet the special needs of your own community.

In the next chapter we will describe several models of day care centers in the United States. Again we advise you to look carefully at each and then decide what components best fit your particular needs.

# CHAPTER THREE

# Infant Day Care in America

Most group infant day-care programs in the New World have been in operation for less than a decade; consequently they are far less uniform than their Old World counterparts. Such infant programs range in scope from high-powered experimental projects to minimal facilities offering only custodial care.

In our survey we have tried to select centers representing a variety of optimal care arrangements for infants. We have included several experimental projects and five child-care service models. Both groups offer a tremendous range in type of program and services. The primary goal for most experimental projects, however, has been intervention and cognitive stimulation for lower-class "deprived" infants rather than direct provision of comprehensive quality day-care services. Such experimental projects are designed to offer infants highly individualized attention for part of each day.

Many child-care service centers attempt to duplicate the mother-child pattern in the home by providing individualized care. Other centers emphasize social adjustment and group activities. The search for methods of readjusting patterns of child rearing seems to reflect the attempt of many modern parents to find alternative and perhaps better methods of integrating and preparing their children for life in our highly complex industrialized society.

We have not attempted to discuss all infant day-care projects in the New World. Such a discussion would be repetitious and tedious. Instead, we have selected representative examples of various infant-care programs—both recent experimental projects and child-care service centers now in operation. We have limited our discussion of infant day care to representative half-day and full-day programs providing learning experiences for children in groups.

We have omitted specialized day care centers for children who are physically handicapped, mentally retarded, and/or emotionally disturbed. Research has not determined whether such infants would be better off integrated with normal children or segregated in groups of comparable ability. In all probability, the decision will depend not only on the individual child but also on the capability of personnel of individual day care centers to provide any necessary specialized care.

We have also ignored day care centers which offer only custodial care. Infancy is such an important period in life that such minimal programs offer little prospect of fulfilling a child's needs, and may in fact be detrimental.

Finally, we have omitted projects designed to provide tutoring for mothers and infants in their own homes, since they do not fall within our definition of infants cared for in groups.


## DEMONSTRATION RESEARCH PROJECT MODELS

### 1. *THE CHILDREN'S CENTER*
Syracuse University
Syracuse, New York
Present Director: Ronald Lally
Past Director: Bettye Caldwell

*Description*
One of the oldest infant day care centers, the Children's Center, was established in the fall of 1964 at Syracuse University. Bettye Caldwell was the first director of the center for seventy-five children ranging from six months to five years in age. About one-third of the children at the center were classified as infants, i.e., under the age of two. It had a total of eight classrooms, a kitchen, and a gym, as well as necessary office space.

The original goal of the Children's Center was one of research and demonstration. The principal objective was the development of an intervention day-care program for very young children from predominantly "deprived" backgrounds.

While the original goals have not been altered significantly under the present director, several changes have occurred, including the development of a training program for personnel working with infants and "family," or mixed-age, groups, rather than groupings by strict chronological age.

### Program

Individualized attention for each infant is provided by assigning one adult to work with the same babies every day. Concepts are emphasized—big, little, large, soft, late—as teachers verbalize constantly for children. Infants are handled with warmth and affection, and receive much stimulation and attention. Children are allowed to choose materials as they desire, while teachers are encouraged to suggest stimulating activities.

Some program goals for children are: the development of a good self-image; a sense of mastery, trust, autonomy; and cognitive, emotional, and social development appropriate for their age.

### Group Size and Adult-Child Ratio

There are approximately fifteen children in each group. For infants under the age of three, the center maintains a ratio of one adult for every four children.

### Staff

In the infant group (six to twelve months), all teachers are registered nurses. After infancy, toddlers are placed in mixed-age groups (eighteen to forty-two months) under the direction of one head and one "co" head teacher and several assistant teachers. Head teachers are experienced instructors who have had some training in early-childhood education. Preference is given to "co" and assistant teachers who have an associate degree in child development, but a degree is not essential if the person displays a general ability to work with young children.

All teaching staff receive intensive training in working with infants. Major areas covered in the training program include a basic understanding of sensory-motor development; the use of appropriate learning materials; and the formulation of a variety of activities appropriate to each developmental age and stage in childhood. Only persons who like young children and demonstrate an ability to work with them are considered appropriate teachers for such infants.

*Cost*
There is a sliding-scale fee schedule, with $5 per week the median rate charged.

*Research Evaluation*
Two-thirds of the children at the center come from low-income families, while the remaining one-third are from middle-income environments. A control group selected from the same basic population strata is being tested as a basis of comparison.

Tests are administered in the fall and spring of each year. The following testing measures are employed for research purposes:

1. Cattell Infant Intelligence Test (1 month-3 years)
2. Stanford-Binet (2 years-16 years)
3. ITPA (2½ years-        )
4. Early Language Assessment Scale (5 months-        )
5. Developmental Checklist.

Results indicate that middle-income children at the center make more rapid IQ gains than do lower-income children; but the IQ scores of both groups continue to rise, while the IQ scores of children in the control group actually decrease, according to this study.

## 2. DEMONSTRATION PROGRAM IN INFANT CARE AND EDUCATION
Ontario, Canada
Director: William Fowler

*Description*
The Demonstration Program in Infant Care and Education is a research project designed to study infants between the ages of two and thirty months, and to develop appropriate teaching materials for infants and an adequate training program for the staff.

The study-group infants are enrolled in a Mother-craft Nursery which provides full-day care. The nursery is housed in a large, reconverted house which contains both playrooms and sleeping rooms as well as office space and observation facilities. Adjoining the house is an outdoor area where the children enjoy outdoor play.

### Program
In addition to group activities, daily individual tutorial learning sessions are provided for every child. Sensory-motor development is emphasized; and the cognitive skills of problem solving, language acquisition, and perception are stressed.

### Group Size and Adult-Child Ratio
There are twenty-five babies in the infant center. The ratio is one adult to two or three children.

### Staff
The Mother-craft staff consists of a nurse teacher-director, one nursery-school teacher, and four assistant teachers. In addition, students from a school of practical nursing assist at the center.

### Research Evaluation
Twenty advantaged middle-class and five disadvantaged inner-city children and their matched controls are being followed in this study. Measures used to test for differences include Bayley Mental Scales and Uzgiris-Hunt Scales.

Research findings to date indicate the younger an infant enters the nursery program, the more substantial is his IQ gain, and show a significant IQ improvement for the nursery children compared to those cared for exclusively at home.

### 3. DEMONSTRATION PROJECT IN GROUP CARE FOR INFANTS
University of North Carolina
Greensboro, North Carolina
Director: Mary Keister

### Description
A demonstration project in group care for infants was established at Greensboro, North Carolina, during the summer of 1967. The program enrolled children aged three to twenty-four

months. The orientation of the project was not cognitive; its goal was simply to demonstrate that group care for infants is no worse than family care.

The infant center was located in a church school near the university. In addition to four classrooms, there were a kitchen, sickroom, and office space.

### Program
This infant center did not have a high-powered intervention program component. Instead, an attempt was made to reproduce the warm, relaxed atmosphere of a good home environment. Infants were allowed to choose toys to play with from a rich assortment. Babies not yet walking were placed in jump seats where they could play with their own toys and at the same time watch the older children.

### Group Size and Adult-Child Ratio
Twenty-two babies ranging in age from three to twenty-four months were divided into three groups, one group consisting of twelve 3- to 18-month-old infants and two groups of toddlers, one 15 to 20 months and another 20 to 24 months. The adult-child ratio was one to four.

### Staff
All nursery caretakers were mothers who, except for a brief four-day orientation session, were trained on the job. Administrative tasks were handled by the nursery director and her associate, while the medical component was supervised by a part-time nurse.

### Hours of Operation
The center provides full-day care from 8:00 A.M. to 5:30 P.M. weekdays (holidays excluded), twelve months a year.

### Cost
There is a sliding-scale fee ranging from $1 to $15 per week, based on family income.

### Associated Services
Part-time pediatric and social worker services are available at the center. The pediatrician is on call daily and consults with

the staff twice a week. The part-time social worker consults with staff and parents whenever necessary.

*Research Evaluation*

Babies and toddlers in the center were paired with home babies, matched by age, sex, race, education of parents, and birth order. The following measures were used to assess development:

1. Bayley Infant Development Scales
2. Stanford-Binet
3. Uzgiris-Hunt Scale
4. Vineland Social Maturity Scale
5. Preschool Attainment Records.

Results indicated no substantial differences between the nursery and control infants as measured by these instruments.

4. *THE TREMONT STREET INFANT CENTER*

Boston, Massachusetts

Co-Principal Investigators: Jerome Kagan, Richard Kearsley

*Description*

The Tremont Street Infant Center was established in order to study and compare the development of infants in a day-care program with a matched group of infants reared exclusively in the home, and to test the effectiveness of certain intervention techniques designed to stimulate cognitive development.

The center is divided into one infant classroom, one isolation room, a small utility kitchen, observation room, conference area, reception area, testing rooms, and several large offices.

*Program*

In addition to regular care in the group, each infant receives a one-to-one session with the same teacher daily. During these sessions the infant is presented with certain games and experiences described in the training manual in order to study the infants' responses to intervention techniques, and measure how much they can be helped by these procedures.

Only Chinese children are involved in both experimental and control groups. First- or second-born infants enter the program at three and a half months of age and remain for a period of ten months while participating in the study.

### Group Size and Adult-Child Ratio
At full capacity there are sixteen Chinese children in both the experimental nursery and control home groups. A ratio of one adult to four infants is maintained for the group of day-care infants.

### Staff
The two principal investigators, a psychologist, and a pediatrician, direct the program. In addition, there is a head teacher, four full-time teachers, a community consultant, secretary, and a maintenance man. The head teacher is a secondary school teacher, and the nursery teachers are women of the community who have received in-service training by the principal investigators in use of the infant curriculum manual.

### Hours of Operation
The Infant Center is open from 8:00 A.M. to 4:30 P.M., Monday through Friday.

### Cost
There is no charge for infants enrolled in the research project. The study is supported by a project grant from the National Institute of Child Health and Human Development, as well as a grant from the Carnegie Corporation of New York.

### Associated Services
The project pediatrician examines each infant accepted for study. He is available as a consultant for any medical matters pertaining to infant health needs. The community consultant assists parents to make use of community resources.

### Research Evaluation
The experimental Chinese nursery infants and their matched controls are evaluated every two months. In addition to the standard Bayley Developmental Scale, each infant is presented

with special evaluation procedures in serial episodes. These procedures are designed to test the effectiveness of the training manual, which has been designed to increase the infant's awareness of variations in his environment.

Since the program has been in operation only since June, 1971, no data concerning its effectiveness are available at this time.

## 5. *THE FRANK PORTER GRAHAM CHILD DEVELOPMENT CENTER*

Chapel Hill, North Carolina

Present Directors: Marjorie Land, Joseph Sparling

Past Director: Halbert Robinson

### Description

The Frank Porter Graham Child Developmental Center, when completed, will have an enrollment of 240 preschool children. Plans for study include longitudinal follow-up for such children from birth through the age of twelve. There is a matched control group of children being reared at home who are also being followed. Classrooms are located in a complex of trailers, which also provide space for offices and curriculum resources.

### Program

Children are placed in mixed-age groupings of fifteen or sixteen per trailer. Special programs for children grouped by chronological age are scheduled for one hour in the morning and again in the afternoon. In addition, there is a structured individual session in language development for infants and toddlers.

### Group Size and Adult-Child Ratio

Children are placed in mixed-age groupings of fifteen or sixteen with three adult caretakers—a ratio of one adult for every five children.

### Staff

There are three categories of staff personnel. The caretakers are primarily community women who have received brief in-service training sessions. Special teachers working with groups of children on specific curriculums have a B.A. or equivalent degree. Curriculum specialists having at least an M.A. design the various teaching programs for the children.

### Hours of Operation
The center provides full-day care from 8:00 A.M. to 5:30 P.M. five days a week.

### Research Evaluation
Children for both the experimental and matched control groups are recruited prior to birth from a nearby prenatal clinic. Both groups receive health and medical care and are tested at intervals using the Bayley Mental and Motor Scales.

Preliminary reports seem to indicate that the day-care group of infants is maintaining satisfactory intellectual and motor development.

### 6. PROJECT KNOW-HOW
Tallahassee, Florida
Director: Richard Dunham

### Description
In Project Know-How, twenty-six infants aged thirteen to twenty-six months, from lower-economic families, attend a half-day preschool program five days a week. At present there are two center locations, each housed in a single-story two-bedroom duplex dwelling. The project plans to accept thirty additional children each year.

### Program
In addition to traditional nursery school group activities, the infants receive individual tutoring in language development by "verbalizers" who work with each child daily on a one-to-one basis for about twenty minutes. The project's major emphasis seems to be to work with the parents to aid in dealing with problems in their own lives.

### Group Size and Adult-Child Ratio
The thirteen children at each center have two professional

teachers in charge of program activities. In addition, mothers assist the teachers so that the adult-child ratio is usually one to two.

### Staff

The four professional teachers are assisted by two verbalizers who work individually with the children in language development.

### Research Evaluation

The twenty-six children are evaluated by the Schaefer Language Development Checklist and Bayley Infant Scale.

Plans are in the offing to include two matching control groups, but at present there are insufficient data for any conclusions about the effectiveness of the day-care program.

## CHILD CARE SERVICE MODELS FOR INFANT CARE

1. *CRISPUS ATTUCKS CHILDREN'S CENTER*
   Formerly: *AVCO Roxbury Day-Care Center*
   Boston, Massachusetts 02121
   Director: Sally Jarvis

### Description

The AVCO Printing and Publishing Company has sponsored a day care center on its premises. Eligible participants included both children of employees and other children living in the Roxbury-Dorchester community. A recent merger with the Crispus Attucks Day Care Center has increased the enrollment at AVCO, which at full capacity has sixty-five children from three months old to five years.

The center is located on the second floor of the AVCO printing plant. Folding partitions divide the area into three separate rooms segregating each group: the infant-toddlers; the two- and young three-year-olds; and the preschool group of three- to five-year-olds.

### Program

The program is highly structured because the staff believes it is very important to prepare the children for public school.

Teacher-directed learning activities include reading and number readiness in the two-year-old and preschool groups. The two- through five-year-olds are subjected to an adult-directed learning experience. Only in the infant-toddler group are children allowed to engage in spontaneous activities for most of the day.

### Group Size and Adult-Child Ratio

The center divides the children into three groups, as follows:

1. Infant-toddler (3 to 24 months), with two adults to eleven infants, a ratio of one to five plus
2. Two-year-olds (2½ to 3 years), with one male teacher to ten children, a ratio of one to ten
3. Preschool (3 to 5 years), with two teachers to eighteen children, a ratio of one to nine

### Staff

The center's director is a professional teacher who holds a master's degree in early-childhood education. She is responsible for supervising the paraprofessional community teachers.

In addition to paid staff, student teachers from nearby colleges and universities come to the center at least eight hours per week per student.

### Hours of Operation

The center is open from 7:30 A.M. to 6:00 P.M. (5:30 P.M. during winter), Monday through Friday.

### Cost

Present costs are $40 to $50 per child per week, depending on the age of the child. Younger children cost more than older children because of the larger adult-child ratio. The AVCO company paid the entire initial cost of establishing the program, and subsidizes 44 percent of operating costs, including rent, utilities, maintenance, and use of the company cafeteria.

There is a fee of $15 per week per child charged to families of both employees and nonemployees alike. For the third child in a family, and every child thereafter, the fee is reduced to $10 per week per additional child.

### Associated Services

The plant nurse is available throughout the day, and supervises the health of children at the center. Children receive two hot meals a day, prepared in the company cafeteria, plus a snack. In addition, there are periodic visits to the center by a state social worker, a psychiatrist, a pediatrician, and personnel from the Tufts Dental School.

## 2. BROMLEY HEATH INFANT CENTER
Jamaica Plain, Massachusetts
Director: Louise Bowditch

### Description

The Bromley Heath Infant Center was opened in May 1971 to provide full-day care to twenty-one children of A.F.D.C. (Aid for Families of Dependent Children) recipients residing in the Bromley Heath Housing Project. The infants' age range is from 3 months to 2⅔ years.

The infant center is located on the first floor of two adjoining apartments in the project. There are six separate rooms—two for sleeping, two for activities, one kitchen and one laundry.

### Program

In addition to normal child-care activities, infants receive daily one-to-one periods of structured play in accordance with recommendations of an infant curriculum designed by "experts." Teachers submit monthly reports assessing each child's progress.

### Group Size and Adult-Child Ratio

There are five staff members for twenty-one children, a ratio of one to four.

### Staff

The staff consists of five paid members, including a director with a master's degree in early-childhood education, and four New Careers teacher-trainee paraprofessionals. Volunteers from nearby colleges and universities assist at the center.

*Hours of Operation*
The infant center is open from 8:00 A.M. to 6:00 P.M. Monday through Friday.

*Cost*
$52 per child per week is paid by the Department of Public Welfare.

*Associated Services*
Medical and social services are available at the Bromley Heath Health Center located within the project. A visiting nurse comes to the center once a week to talk with teachers and assess infants' health needs. Children's Hospital provides emergency care and consultant psychiatric services.

### 3. *CASTLE SQUARE DAY CARE CENTER*
Boston, Massachusetts
Director: E. Belle Evans

*Description*
In 1969 the Department of Public Health Division of Family Health Services established a Career Development Laboratory to train in child-care educationally disadvantaged men and women referred from the Boston offices of WIN (Work Incentive). In order to have a laboratory school for teacher training, the division opened a small storefront nursery school in the Castle Square Housing Project.

A year later, in response to the needs of the community, the Division of Family Health Services expanded the nursery school program into a full day care center for fifty-two children from the Castle Square neighborhood. Additional need for child care resulted in another expansion to the present enrollment of 130 children, ranging from one month to six years of age. Seventy-two of these children are under the age of three years, since this is the age group with the greatest need for child-care services.

The majority of the children at the center are members of families receiving Aid for Families of Dependent Children. Preference is given to children living in the Castle Square Housing Project. In addition, six scholarships are available for children who live in the Castle Square area but are not registered under A.F.D.C. As part of their fringe benefits, members of the staff are permitted to enroll their children in the program. They are assessed on a sliding-scale basis to help repay the center for the cost of this service.

Children are assigned on the basis of age to the six class-rooms—an infant center for babies one to twenty months; a toddler room for children aged eighteen to thirty months; a room for young two-year-olds; a room for children not quite three and young three-year-olds; a room for more advanced three-year-olds and young four-year-olds; and, finally, a room for advanced four-year-olds and five-year-olds.

The day care center occupies the first-floor storefront space in the Castle Square Housing Project. The center is divided into five major areas: six classrooms for children; a joint activity room for water play, climbing, swings, and wheeled vehicles; a kitchen; an isolation room; and an office area. Additional space for workshops and teacher-training classrooms is provided.

### Program
Children are grouped according to developmental abilities. Both the classroom environment and the daily programs are de-signed to meet the needs of the specific children in each group.

Each child is recognized as a unique individual with enor-mous capacities for growth and development. Through group and individual activities, each child is encouraged to develop at his own rate in his own way. By providing a rather unstruc-tured educational environment the staff believe they are ensur-ing the best possible development of each child.

### Group Size and Adult-Child Ratio
The Castle Square Day Care Center follows the Federal Interagency Guidelines for staff ratio to group size. Hence, one adult is assigned to serve the needs of four infants under the age of 2¾ years; for three-year-olds the ratio is increased to one to five; for four-year-olds it is one to six; and for five-year-olds it reaches one to seven.

### Staff
The staff of the Castle Square Day Care Center consists of seven administrators, twenty-six teachers, two kitchen workers,

and two maintenance men. The director is a nurse who also holds a master's degree in early-childhood education. She directs both the day-care and preschool teacher-training programs conducted at the center. The child-care supervisor is an experienced teacher with a master's degree in education. She is in charge of program operations at the day care center. The training supervisor is in charge of the preschool teacher-training program conducted at the day care center for Work Incentive (WIN). She is working toward her master's degree in early-childhood education. Other members of the administrative staff include an administrative assistant, a social worker, a nutritionist (part-time), and a secretary/receptionist.

The majority of the teaching staff are graduates of the preschool teacher-training program conducted at the center. The director and two other staff members at the center hold faculty appointments at Wheelock College. Therefore, the WIN teacher-trainees receive thirty college credits for the courses taught at the center. In addition, there are several community teaching staff members. Formal educational credentials are considered less important than the basic ability to relate and to work with young children.

In addition to twenty-four WIN preschool teacher-trainees, volunteers and student teachers from nearby colleges and universities contribute at least eight hours per week per person to the day care center.

### Hours of Operation
The center is open from 8:00 A.M. to 5:30 P.M., Monday through Friday.

### Cost
The Department of Public Welfare pays $56 per week per child for children under the age of three years, and $40 per week per child for children three- to five-years-old.

### Associated Services
A pediatrician visits the day care center every other week to perform routine physical examinations, and give immunizations to the children. Once a month he meets with teachers to discuss child growth and development. The director is a registered nurse and is responsible for basic first-aid procedures and

supervising the health component at the day care center. Emergency care and treatment of injuries are provided by Beth Israel Hospital. Screening programs are provided at the center to discover evidence of lead poisoning, and vision, speech, and hearing defects.

In conjunction with Tufts Dental School, a dental program has been developed which includes prophylactic topical fluoride applications, routine cleanings and checkups, together with dental treatment. A dental student conducts a program for children, teachers, and parents, emphasizing the need for good mouth hygiene and preventive dental care.

Social services are provided by a community social worker responsible for helping both the children and their parents with individual and family problems, so they are able to make best use of available community resources and services.

Under the supervision of the nutritionist, children are fed breakfast, lunch, and two snacks per day. Infants receive formulas and solid feedings as prescribed by the pediatrician.

A psychologist visits the center twice a month to meet with staff and discuss how to handle behavior problems. He examines individual children who display unusual symptoms, and may recommend referral for special treatment.

### 4. *NATIONAL CAPITAL AREA DAY CARE CENTER*
14th and Indiana Avenue, N.W.
Washington, D.C.
Director: Audrey Gibson

*Description*
The day care center is operated by the National Capital Area Day Care Association for children of Department of Labor employees. The center enrolls about sixty children, ranging in age from nineteen months to five years. Ten children, aged nineteen to thirty months, are assigned to the infant program. The center is located on the first floor of the Auditor's Building, and houses four classrooms, an office, a meeting room, kitchen, lavatory, and a food-snack storage room.

*Program*
The program is comprehensive, aimed at fostering each child's intellectual, physical, emotional, and social development.

Both Bank Street and Science Research Associates materials are used to encourage language development and the acquisition of the tools of learning, that is, gathering, organizing, and processing information.

### Group Size and Adult-Child Ratio

In the infant program, one adult is assigned to four children, for whom she is responsible. Fifteen children, aged 2½ to 3½ years, are cared for by one teacher and her two assistants, a ratio of one adult to five children.

### Staff

The director of the center is a college graduate with many years' teaching experience. All four teachers have bachelor degrees in child development or education, while the three assistant teachers have had training in child care. The center also employs two teacher aides and several part-time personnel, including two New Career trainees, a social worker, a nurse, a psychiatric consultant, a clerk aide, a maintenance aide, a music teacher, and a speech teacher.

### Hours of Operation

The center is open from 7:30 A.M. to 6:00 P.M., Monday through Friday.

### Cost

Parents are charged for day-care services according to a sliding scale based on family income. The Department of Labor subsidizes the center as a fringe benefit to its employees. The cost ranges from $1 per week per child for families with an annual family income under $4,000 to $30 per week per child for a family earning $17,000 per year.

### Associated Services

A social worker comes to the center two and one-half days a week; she conducts weekly meetings with parents, and is available on an individual basis to parents who may need her services.

A psychiatrist visits the center two afternoons per week to observe children, and to consult with both parents and staff.

A nurse is available in case of emergency, and also to help

families get adequate medical and dental care. She is responsible for keeping up-to-date medical records for each child and informing parents of screenings and medical tests given at the center.

Children receive two hot meals a day in addition to morning and afternoon snacks.

The child-care center sponsored by the Department of Labor is a comprehensive unit providing optimal care for children. It is an example of an employer-sponsored program providing for the needs of all concerned. The children receive quality day care; the parents, both employment and a wholesome environment for their children; and the employer, a stable work force who appreciate this fringe benefit.

## EVALUATION

Group infant day care in the United States is in the pioneering stage. Recently several studies have tested the effects of group care on infants, but a complete scientific comparison of results for day care infants versus matched home controls is impossible because much data are fragmentary or unavailable at the present time. Preliminary findings seem to indicate, however, that infants involved in quality group care do no worse than infants cared for exclusively at home, and in most cases they obtain higher scores on standard IQ tests.

While we personally feel that infants in day care are provided with many more opportunities for stimulation and social development, we are uncomfortable with standard intelligence tests used to measure differences. There is no general agreement on exactly what such IQ tests are measuring. Moreover, many authorities feel IQ tests are designed for middle-class children and therefore should not be used when testing children from other socioeconomic backgrounds.

If one assumes that IQ tests are valid measuring devices, it would seem that infants in group day care benefit from the stimulus of more attention and the broader horizons of their environment. It appears that middle-class children benefit more from group care than lower-class children. Moreover, the findings seem to indicate that the younger a child when exposed to a stimulating environment the faster his development. In short, if one were to make an evaluation on the basis of available information both from this and other countries, one must conclude that quality group infant day care is a positive experience for children, one which encourages and stimulates physical, intellectual, psychological, and social development.

Although some authorities feared that day care programs would develop "institutionalized" children, all the studies indicate that such fears were groundless in relation to quality day care centers. It might be a different story in the case of centers offering only custodial care. As indicated previously, we have omitted centers of this type from our consideration, and we know of no scientific study attempting to discover the effects of minimal day-care facilities on infants.

Far more relevant for study, in our opinion, are quality day care centers not associated directly with research efforts. These centers range in scope from highly structured establishments (basically adult oriented) to child-centered programs attempting to encourage each child to develop in his own way at his own rate. The type of center one prefers depends upon several circumstances:

- The personality and abilities of the individual child
- The wishes and needs of the child's parents
- The kind of teaching personnel available
- The expertise of the administrative staff
- The basic philosophy of the center itself

Proponents of the "structured" system believe that lower-class children need the security of order and discipline; often the center represents the only stabilizing influence in their otherwise disorganized lives. Many centers are giving such children excellent preparation for future learning experiences in the typical urban school.

We tend to shy away from such rigidity since we believe that this approach stifles initiative and creativity. However, we are aware that a structured curriculum may be necessary for helping some children, at least until they have learned to discipline themselves.

We believe that quality infant group care can provide a reasonable alternative to exclusive home care. Our own son,

Evan, has been in day care since he was one month old, and we are very pleased with his normal and even somewhat precocious development. For us, quality infant day care has provided the alternative we desired, and we strongly advocate that such an alternative choice be made available to other parents. Our feelings of confidence in quality day care were reinforced by observing long-established programs in other countries as well as by the success of the many small pilot projects undertaken more recently in this country. Whether or not such centers will expand and proliferate will depend on interest expressed in word and deed by people seeking to provide or utilize similar child day-care arrangements. In succeeding chapters we describe what, in our opinion, makes a quality day care center. We hope our advice will be helpful. Again, we stress our belief that quality day care centers should be available to all parents who want them.

We believe that all day care centers should—

1. attempt to meet the needs of each individual child for maximum physical, intellectual, psychological, and social growth;
2. develop a program which will best meet the desires and needs of the parents and the community it serves;
3. make the best possible use of all available resources;
4. realize that perfection is unobtainable, but that progress is achieved by doing the best possible job with the resources available.

## PART TWO

# Guide to Starting and Operating an Infant Day Care Center

## INTRODUCTION

In the following chapters we will describe what we feel constitutes a quality infant-care program. Whether you are interested in expanding an existing center to include infants, attempting to develop a new center, wishing to evaluate an existing center with the intention of enrolling your child, or interested in new ideas and procedures in working with children, we hope you will find our description both informative and helpful in a practical way.

Because each state has different rules, regulations, and restrictions for licensing group infant day care, it will be necessary for you to check requirements in your state. To help you acquire an overall view, we have described and summarized some existing standards. Far more useful, in all probability, will be Appendix A, which should help you find the licensing agency in your own state.

After you have become familiar with laws regarding group infant care in your state, you can begin to solve the problems of preparing a budget and securing funds to operate your program; finding and developing a suitable site and obtaining the necessary permits for licensing your center; staffing your center with quality personnel; providing appropriate toys and equipment—in short, devising and implementing a comprehensive child-care program for infants. We hope you will find our survey interesting and informative, whatever your individual needs or purpose may be.

CHAPTER FOUR

# Licensing Requirements

Before you attempt to set up a day care center you must know the ground rules. Most states have regulations setting minimum standards for the operation of day care centers. The licensing agents in each state inspect new centers before granting an official permit to operate and conduct annual inspections for license renewal. Since licensing requirements vary from state to state, you will need to obtain a copy of the rules and regulations for day care centers in your state.

The Department of Welfare has primary licensing responsibility in most states, but in some states it is shared jointly with the Department of Health, or may be assumed completely by some other state agency, such as the Department of Education. See Appendices, pages 144–145, for a listing by state of the licensing agencies. Obviously you should contact the appropriate agency in your state first, so that you will develop both your center and its program in compliance with the state code.

In some states infants are not accepted legally in group day-care arrangements. If this is true in your state, we strongly recommend that you bring this inadequacy to the attention of your state legislators. We know that in such states infants are receiving care in illegal, unlicensed homes and centers. If these children are to be protected, minimum standards of care must be established. Moreover—a fact of vital concern to you as an organizer—you will not be able to receive any federal money if your state has not established acceptable standards for infant day care and some mechanism for inspection and certification that ensures that these standards are being maintained. If your state has already formulated rules and regulations for group care of infants, get a copy of the requirements, so the program you develop will at least comply with minimum standards. If your state has not established guidelines, your first task must be to form a citizens' committee to lobby for the enactment of standards.

Regulations, wherever they do exist, are usually quite specific concerning safety, building, and health requirements. While these standards may help you develop a safe environment for children, they contain little assistance or guidance for your actual program operation. For this reason it will be up to the organizer to develop the content of your program in compliance with the needs of your children and the wishes of their parents. Actually this is a blessing in disguise, since it will enable you to develop a day care center that will best meet the needs of your own community.

We have included seven examples to illustrate the scope of the regulations, as well as show the variety of interpretation from state to state. Our list includes the following:

1. A definition of what is meant by infant day care
2. Exemptions for any organizations or agencies not subject to licensing requirements
3. The number and age of infants allowed in a group
4. The ratio of infants to an adult caretaker
5. The minimum age and qualifications for adults caring for infants in a group setting
6. Building restrictions, such as construction location
7. Specified square-foot-per-child allowances for both indoor and outdoor areas

While we limit our discussion to these seven areas, each state has very specific guidelines for other aspects of the program. These procedures vary widely from state to state. Again we must warn you to consult your state standards for infant care. Make the state regulations your guidebook. Read and reread them. Lobby for their improvement, so that the quality of day care may be improved also.

1. *Definition*
*Infants* and *infant day care centers* are defined differently in each state. In most states, however, infants are classified as those children under the age of three years, and day care centers

are designated as those places caring for a group of infants outside their own homes.

## 2. Exemptions

In some states certain programs are exempt from licensing. Examples include: educational institutions; state owned and controlled institutions; social, medical, or recreational-type programs; programs operated by religious organizations, such as Sunday schools. Check the exemptions which apply to your state.

## 3. Number and Age of Infants Allowed in a Group

State requirements vary in the number of children allowed in a group before the program comes under licensing law. For example, in Massachusetts, if there are three or more children not of common parentage being cared for by someone other than their parents, such an arrangement is defined as group care and subject to licensing. At the other extreme, a group of as many as fifteen infants can be cared for in North Carolina before such a program is subject to licensing practices.

The age of infants admitted to a program is also subject to wide variation. Connecticut allows infants of one month to be enrolled in group care, whereas in other states children under three years are generally not allowed in group care. To date the following states fall in this category: Indiana, Kansas, Massachusetts, Missouri, Nebraska, New Hampshire, Pennsylvania, Rhode Island, and Wyoming. As yet other states do not allow group care for infants under the age of two.

Be sure to check the rules in your state regarding group infant care. Again, if your state presently does not allow infant day care, lobby to change such antiquated laws. According to the Department of Labor statistics, 30 percent of mothers with preschool children are now working. During the last twenty years the number of working mothers has doubled (22 percent in 1950, 42 percent in 1970). The prospect is that this trend will continue in the future.

## 4. Adult-Child Ratio

While the number of children that may be cared for by one adult varies from a low of two infants in Nevada to a high of ten infants in Arizona, Minnesota, New Mexico, and Oregon, most states require one adult caretaker for every four infants. See Appendices, pages 146–147, for a listing by state and age of the maximum number of infants which may be cared for by one adult. While your state may allow a higher child-adult ratio, in our opinion quality care cannot be achieved if the ratio rises above four infants under the age of three years for each adult.

### 5. Staff Qualifications

Most states do not have stringent requirements for adults who care for children. A high school diploma or equivalent experience is usually all that is required for the teaching staff, although the director often needs some college credits or a few years' experience in caring for young children.

The minimum age for both teachers and directors ranges from a low of age sixteen in Iowa to a high of twenty-one in most other states. In our experience, our most successful teachers have been more mature and experienced than the minimum standard required by law, and we advise you to read carefully our suggestions for selecting child-care personnel, which we shall discuss in chapter 8, "Staffing Your Program."

### 6. Building Restrictions

Often states have stringent building requirements for programs involving young children. Most states stipulate that day care centers be located on the ground or first floor, so the building can be readily evacuated in case of emergency. In addition, inspection is usually required for electrical and plumbing systems as well as general building construction. Some states will not allow centers to be housed in wood frame buildings. Again, be sure to check the building requirements in your state before selecting a location for your center.

### 7. Square-Foot-per-Child Space Allowances

In addition to building construction restrictions, most states insist on minimal space allocations for child-care programs. These apply to both indoor as well as outdoor space. Such space requirements will set the maximum number of children your center may enroll. Indoor space requirements do not vary dramatically among states. Maine and Virginia require only twenty square feet of space for each child, but most states require thirty-five square feet per child. We believe that thirty-five square feet should be a minimum allotment, especially for active toddlers who need room for large-muscle activities.

The range in minimal space requirements for outdoor area is enormous—from a low of forty square feet per child in Florida and Utah to a high of two hundred square feet per child in Wyoming. While most states recommend seventy-five square feet per child, we feel that for active young children a minimum of one hundred square feet per child is more realistic.

Most states require that outdoor play space be fenced in, especially if the center is located on a busy street or is hazardous for some other reason. For very young children who lack both conscience and controls, fencing is absolutely necessary, both to ensure safety and to facilitate proper supervision.

SUMMARY

State rules and regulations establish standards for licensing group infant-care programs, and provide minimum guidelines to ensure that adequate care is given. While specific requirements vary from state to state, most states attempt, by licensing, to insure that standards are met in the areas of safety, fire, health, sanitation, and programming. We have given only a few examples to illustrate the wide variation in regulations. You must secure a copy of the rules and regulations from your own state in order to develop a feasible plan for implementing your specific program.

After reading the licensing requirements of your state carefully, you should follow this procedure: formulate a budget and secure a funding mechanism for your proposed program; select and develop a potential site in accordance with state regulations; apply for a license to operate your program from the state licensing agency; obtain inspection permits as necessary from the city building inspectors, environmental health inspector, and fire inspector; obtain a zoning permit or file for a zoning variance; hire your teaching staff; design your classroom environment; recruit your children; submit health records of both staff and children for medical assessment if necessary; and finally receive your license to operate a day care center enrolling infants. In succeeding chapters we shall discuss these steps in great detail.

CHAPTER FIVE

# Preparing a Budget and Raising Funds

Once you are familiar with the rules and regulations pertaining to infant day care in your state and you have decided it is feasible to continue, raising funds will be your next challenging problem. Whether you are a group of students attempting to interest your college in establishing a day care center, parents trying to begin a small parent cooperative, or organizers of a large day care center desiring to expand by including infant care, funding will be a major consideration.

"Grub stake" (initial funding) money is often the most difficult to get because, although many individuals and agencies do not hesitate to contribute to an existing center, they are reluctant to finance initial costs for a new center.

In this chapter we discuss possible sources for both initial funding and direct program operation. In addition, we will show you how to develop a budget and prepare proposals to funding sources.

## FUNDING SOURCES

Obtaining Initial Capital

The largest stumbling block to establishing a new day care center is often the difficulty in obtaining the funds for the selection and development of a site; fixed costs during the developmental phase (rent or mortgage, electricity, heat, water, staff salaries, and so on); and purchase of necessary initial equipment and supplies.

The actual amount of initial capital outlay will naturally depend upon the number of children you hope to serve, site renovation expenses, and the number of staff you employ prior to actually providing day-care services.

If you are just beginning a new center, usually it is wise to incorporate. While the process may vary somewhat from state to state, it means ordinarily that as organizers you need to draw up bylaws and elect several people to serve on your board of directors. If you are incorporating as a nonprofit organization you should file a petition for tax-exempt status. Either a private lawyer or an association such as Legal Aid will advise you regarding the process of incorporation and the procedure of applying for tax-exempt status.

### Contributions

Whether you have incorporated or not, you can attempt to solicit contributions from individuals and businesses within the community in which you hope to develop your center. Sometimes a foundation will furnish one-time grants, so we suggest you consult *The Foundation Directory*, 3d edition, edited by Marianna O. Lewis (New York: Russell Sage Foundation, 1967). This resource should be available in your local library.

### Donations

Sometimes organizations may not be able to contribute money but may be willing to donate space, toys, equipment, or personnel. Be sure to check local churches, universities, hospitals, businesses, and housing authorities for possible free space. Organize collection drives for used toys in your community, and request local storekeepers to donate new or repairable toys and equipment.

### Fund-Raising Drives

While you may never be able to obtain large amounts of money through various fund-raising activities, usually they do provide a fairly reliable source of small amounts of money. Such fund raising might include rummage sales, raffles, bake sales, car washes, bottle and can collections, paper drives, and sponsored dances.

### Loans

As a last resort it may be necessary to take out a loan in order to start your center. Often the bank which has financed your loan will be willing to take on the payroll responsibilities for your center at minimal cost.

Funding Program Operation

Once you have developed your site, you need adequate funding to ensure daily program operation. The largest source of day-care funds at present is the federal government. However, unless your state has developed rules and regulations for infant day care and a licensing authority to ensure that federal standards are met, you will not be able to take advantage of this source of revenue, which may run as high as $56 per week per child under age three.

*Federal Funding*

There are several federal sources for funding day care center operations. While welfare funding is the source most often available, we feel a program funded exclusively with such monies has several severe problems. In the first place studies have shown that children in a mixed socioeconomic environment tend to develop learning skills more rapidly than low-income children segregated from other children.

Secondly, you will not be able to respond to the needs of the whole community if you enroll children from only one subgroup (i.e., welfare).

Third, it will take several months to be reimbursed for child-care services since the Welfare Department pays monthly after the fact; moreover it takes several months before the bureaucratic system gets moving.

Finally, in our opinion the most serious drawback to funding your program entirely by welfare monies is that under the present system as soon as parents complete their training programs, or get better paying jobs and no longer need welfare subsidies, their children are pulled out of the program. There is no alternative unless they can meet the child-care costs by themselves. This is most unlikely unless you have a sliding scale for parent fees and available matching funds to make up the deficits. For this reason there will be a constant turnover of children at your center. Removing a child from his/her group is not only difficult for the child and his parent, but also has a demoralizing effect on the other children and the staff. Constant recruiting of new children to fill vacated welfare slots requires an enormous amount of time which could be spent to better advantage in other areas.

For these reasons we recommend that you avoid funding your center by using welfare monies entirely, if possible. We believe a combination of funding will provide a stronger basis for your program.

The Department of Labor, Women's Bureau, has recently published a booklet entitled *Federal Funds for Day Care Projects,* describing the numerous federally funded day-care programs. In addition, we suggest you consult the book *Catalog of Federal Domestic Assistance* (Executive Office of the President, Office of Management and Budget, Washington, D.C.). Perhaps your program will meet their criteria for funding. Most federal monies for day care come mainly from the following sources:

1. *Social Security Act (Title IV, Part A).* Under the AFDC (Aid to Families with Dependent Children) federal funds are available to partially or fully pay the costs of child care in the following ways:
   a. Seventy-five percent federal matching is available for use in providing child-care services to mothers participating in the Work Incentive Program.
   b. Seventy-five percent federal matching is also available to the states for day-care services for children of mothers who may be classified as "potential" welfare clients because of their low income.
   c. Working welfare mothers may be subsidized for child-care costs considered a necessary work expense.
2. *Social Security Act (Title IV, Part B).* Day care services may be obtained under the child welfare services program whereby grants are made to the State Welfare Departments for child welfare services. Priority is given to low-income mothers, but they need not be welfare recipients.
3. *Economic Opportunities Act (Head Start).* Eighty percent federal matching is available to local community action agencies or other public and private nonprofit agencies for comprehensive day-care services to poverty-level children.

4. *Department of Labor (New Careers Program).* While the New Careers Program funded through the Department of Labor does not pay directly for child-care expenses, it can cut the cost of paying salaries of your teaching staff by providing up to 100 percent (first year) and 50 percent (second year) of the salaries of New Career teaching staff employed at your center. These staff members will be able to work only a half day since they will be taking courses at nearby colleges, also as part of the New Careers program.

5. *Federal Monies for Research and Demonstration Projects.* Funds are available for demonstration day care research projects through the Office of Child Development in Washington, D.C. Write directly to Washington or to your regional Office of Child Development if you think you can conduct such a project.

### Payment of Fees by Parents

Charging parents for child-care services is another way to secure financial support for your center. Since the actual cost for infant day care is very high (about $50 per child per week), most parents will need to pay on a sliding scale computed on the basis of family income. In order to have a sliding scale, however, you must be able to match parents' contributions with other funds to cover your costs.

### Community Chests or Charities

One way to match parent fees is through receiving monies from local charities or community agencies.

### Other Funding Sources

As mentioned previously, under Initial Funding Sources, program operation monies may also be secured from voluntary contributions, donations, and various fund-raising campaigns. In addition, an established day care center may receive special gifts and even endowment bequests.

## HOW TO DEVELOP A BUDGET

In order to apply for funds you must know how to develop a budget and prepare a proposal for support. When preparing a budget, all services and equipment must be subject to cost-accounting practices. For this reason, a budget will not only describe your program but summarize its cost as well.

The major expense in most day-care budgets is staff salaries. The quality of your program will depend primarily on the quality of your staff, and unless your program is a parent cooperative and most of your staff are volunteers, a quality staff costs money. In 1968 the Office of Economic Opportunity in its *Standards & Costs for Day Care* estimated staff expenses would run between 65 percent and 70 percent of total costs. These percentage estimates were based on low salaries for both professionals ($6,600) and preprofessionals ($4,400). A more realistic estimate of approximately 75 percent staff expenditures has been published in a more recent document entitled *A Study in Child Care 1970–1971,* prepared by ABT Associates for the Office of Economic Opportunity. Both estimates are based on child-care programs for three- to five-year-olds where the child-staff ratio is higher than that recommended for infant care. At Castle Square, where children under the age of three years comprise almost one-third of our total enrollment, 84 percent of our budget is spent on staff salaries.

Other budget items include associated services, such as health, nutrition, and social; equipment and supplies; rent and utilities; and other costs, such as travel, insurance, repairs, admission fees to special events. The ABT study estimates that approximately 6 to 7 percent of a day-care budget is spent on foodstuffs, another 9 percent on rent and 9 to 10 percent on all other expenses.

Since the needs of very small programs are quite different from larger ones, we shall discuss these centers separately in chapter 11, "Parent Cooperative Infant Care Centers."

## PERSONNEL COSTS

As we have seen, personnel costs comprise by far the greatest expense of most day-care budgets. The actual composition of the staff in your center will depend upon the number of children you care for, their ages, the staff-child ratio, the need for direct associated services, and the total amount of money you are prepared to spend.

*Administrative Costs*

No matter what the size of your program, some one must take primary responsibility for administration. Smaller centers may not require a full-time director, and, therefore, he/she may also have some teaching responsibilities. Medium-sized centers need a full-time director, and large centers will not only need a full-time director but also an administrative assistant.

Directors' salaries will depend on education and previous experience. We suggest that a professional director, well educated (master's degree in early-childhood education or a related field), and experienced in both working with children and program administration, should receive a salary ranging from $10,000 to $15,000. A preprofessional director without education or supervisory experience might receive half the professional's salary.

Naturally, most directors will be neither of these two extremes, and it will be your responsibility to determine what salary you can afford to pay in order to attract the person you want for this very important position.

While a director and a part-time secretary may be all the administration staff needed in a small center, medium- and large-sized centers will have to increase their administrative personnel to include some or all of the following: a full-time secretary, an administrative assistant, an educational supervisor, and a bookkeeper.

*Teaching Costs*

Of necessity, the largest expenses of any center will be the salaries of its teachers. In chapter 8, "Staffing Your Program," we discuss the need for one experienced head teacher in charge of every classroom. The salaries you pay head teachers will depend on their education and previous experience, and the geographic area in which the center is located. Therefore we suggest that head teachers' salaries should range from $6500 to $9000 depending on these variables.

Assistant teachers may be either educated and experienced or preprofessional. However, we feel that quality personnel deserve a decent salary if they are expected to provide learning experiences for children rather than custodial baby-sitting. Therefore we recommend that no teachers be hired for less than

$5,500. At Castle Square our base salary is $6,000 because the cost of living in Boston is one of the highest in the nation.

The number of teachers you will need depends upon your staff-child ratio. For children younger than three years of age we strongly recommend that you maintain at least a ratio of one to four. Check your rules and regulations in order to be sure you are meeting the minimum requirements in your state. (See Appendices, pages 144–145, "Day Care Licensing by State.") Even in a small center we recommend you try to include a range in age groupings. In this way siblings can attend the same center, even though they are not in the same class. Moreover, this policy helps to maintain a family-type atmosphere rather than a rigid institutional separation by age, as is the custom in some foreign countries (especially in France and Yugoslavia, where up to one hundred infants are kept in separate crèches).

### Auxiliary Personnel Costs

In addition to your administrative and teaching staff, usually you will need auxiliary personnel. Again the number, kind, and cost will depend on the size of your center and how much money you have to spend. Even small centers will need at least a part-time cook and a part-time custodian. Nursing and social service consultation would be very helpful also. Larger centers may require such personnel on a full-time basis, and may add additional auxiliary service personnel as seems necessary. (See chapter 10, "Associated Services.")

### Summary

It should be obvious that personnel costs will vary according to your particular needs and available resources. When computing staff costs, remember to include fringe benefits and administrative costs. Fringe benefits are estimated at 10 percent of salary costs. They must include Social Security and unemployment insurance, and may include medical insurance, sick leave, vacation pay, retirement fund, and workingmen's compensation. The administrative tasks of preparing the payroll and paying bills may be performed by either a hired bookkeeper or accountant, or by contracting with a bank or business to furnish these services. Usually the cost of administering fiscal matters will run between 5 and 10 percent of staff salaries.

*Summary of Suggested Personnel Expenses*

Administrative Staff

| | |
|---|---|
| Director | $7,000-$15,000 |
| Assistant Director | 7,000- 10,000 |
| Administrative Asst. | 6,000- 9,000 |
| Secretary | 5,500- 7,000 |

Teachers

| | |
|---|---|
| Head Teacher | 6,500- 9,000 |
| Assistant Teacher | 5,500- 7,000 |

Associated Services

| | |
|---|---|
| Social Worker | 6,000- 12,000 |
| Pediatric Nurse | 7,000- 9,000 |
| Cook | 5,500- 7,000 |
| Physician Consultant | $100 per day |
| Dentist Consultant | 75 per day |
| Psychologist Consultant | 75 per day |
| Nutritionist | 30 per day |

Maintenance

| | |
|---|---|
| Handyman | 5,000- 7,500 |

## EQUIPMENT COSTS

We have defined equipment costs as those one-time expenditures necessary to equip your office and classrooms. If you are really short of funds, inexpensive homemade equipment can substitute in some cases for more expensive store-bought equivalents. However, you will need access to a workshop and special carpentry equipment if you plan to cut costs by making your office and classroom equipment. Naturally your equipment costs will depend on the size of your center and how effectively you are able to use inexpensive "do-it-yourself" equipment.

*Office Equipment*

A cost comparison between a high-budget allowance for

office equipment and a low-budget substitute might look something like this:

| Equipment Item | High Budget | Low Budget |
| --- | --- | --- |
| Desks for administrative staff | $125 ea. | Homemade, using door or plywood |
| Desk chairs | 40 ea. | $14 |
| Work table for teaching staff | 100 | Homemade |
| Bookcase | 50 | Homemade |
| Stacking or folding chairs for meetings | 14 | $5 (used) |
| Electric typewriter | 500 | 200 (used) |
| Adding machine | 150 | 80 |
| File cabinet | 90 | 25 |
| Cost of materials | | ? |

In order to make a comparison between high and low equipment costs, you will need to multiply each item by the number required in your center.

### Classroom Equipment

Equipment for the classrooms may be homemade or purchased. We began by using mostly homemade curriculum equipment and toys, but soon discovered that many hours of teacher time were spent in repairing and replacing items, rather than in planning learning activities for the children. For this reason we began to replace much of our homemade classroom equipment with more durable, sturdy store-bought items. A comparison of curriculum equipment costs for high and low budgets in both infant and toddler classrooms may be found in the Appendices, pages 151–152, "Sample Budget for 16 Infant Toddlers."

### Carpentry Equipment

In order to make the homemade equipment we have listed in the low-cost budget you will need the following workshop tools:

| | |
|---|---:|
| ¼″ electric drill with assorted drill bits | $30 |
| Electric sander | 25 |
| Framing square | 3 |
| Hammers ( $5 each ) | 15 |
| Saws: circular | 40 |
|       regular | 7 |
|       saber | 30 |
| Screwdrivers, assorted sizes | 10 |
| Tape measures ( $4 each ) | 8 |
| Vise | 12 |
| *Total* | $180 |

## SUPPLIES AND MATERIALS

We define supplies and materials as those items which need periodic replacement in either high- or low-cost budgets. Expenses for supplies will probably cost about the same amount of money.

### Office

Naturally the quantity of office supplies you require will depend on the size of your center and the volume of correspondence. Therefore, the quantity of stationery supplies, such as paper, envelopes, stamps, pens, pencils, typewriter ribbons, tape, staples will be a variable expense you alone can determine.

### Classroom

The majority of classroom supplies and materials can be categorized under the following headings: (1) Caretaking, (2) Clothing, (3) Art, and (4) Housekeeping.

"Suggested Classroom Supplies and Materials," in Appendices, page 150, contains a price list of necessary supplies. Totals will depend on the size of your center.

### Carpentry

If you plan to construct much of your own equipment you will need certain basic materials, as well as tools. The actual amounts of materials will be determined by the size of your center and how much equipment you decide to make. Any list must include:

   Lumber or plywood
   Bolts and nuts (assorted sizes)
   Nails (assorted)
   Screws (assorted sizes)
   Paint ($8 per gallon)
   Plastic varnish ($10 per gallon)
   Sandpaper (assorted grits)

## FOOD SERVICE

Be sure to check the local offices of the National School Lunch Program in your area. As mentioned in chapter 10, "Associated Services," you may be able to receive reimbursement up to three-fourths the cost of equipping your kitchen. Moreover, the School Lunch Program will reimburse you with set amounts per meal per child if your center meets their eligibility requirements. If you cannot meet eligibility standards and must pay the entire foodstuff costs of your center, be sure to allow approximately 7 percent of your budget, or about sixty cents per child per day.

## TRAVEL

Your budget for travel will be very high or very low depending on whether your center provides transportation for children or requires that parents take this responsibility. If you plan to provide transportation, you will need to buy or rent a bus, minibus, or station wagon, and employ a driver. In some small centers the director or a teacher is responsible for picking up and delivering children. We recommend that if you are responsible for providing transportation you should plan to have not only the driver but also one other adult to supervise children. If you provide transportation, the number of children who must be transported will determine the size of the vehicle. For transporting very young children, several minibuses are preferable to one large bus. Rental fees for each minibus cost approximately $200 per month, including repairs and insurance.

Purchasing a bus would probably cost about the same a month.

Even if you do not provide daily transportation, we recommend you have access to transportation services for field trips. In addition, be sure to budget for admission fees, since some supplementary activities do cost money.

Reimbursement of staff for the cost of local field trips to other centers and long-distance travel to conferences and meetings is a good idea if you can afford it.

Thus, the amount of money you must budget for travel expenses will depend upon the following: whether or not your center is responsible for the transportation of children to and from the center, the number of children transported, and the number and extent of field trips provided for both children and staff.

## SPACE COSTS AND UTILITIES

Usually costs for space will run about 6 percent of your total budget. Whether you rent, purchase, or receive donated space, you must be sure to meet the requirements of space per child in your state. (See chapter 4, "Licensing Requirements.")

In addition to space costs you will need to budget for utilities, such as gas, electricity, heat, telephone, water.

## MISCELLANEOUS

Under this catch-all category appear all other costs not previously itemized. They may include repairs, petty cash, and insurance, and the amount budgeted will depend on the needs of your center. We have put together a sample budget using the categories discussed previously. Remember that your actual budget should reflect all the costs of your program and demonstrate how you plan to meet the needs for child care service in your center. (See pages 142–143 for a sample budget.)

## PREPARING A PROPOSAL

Now that you know the sources of funding and how to plan a budget for your program you will need to prepare a proposal to various agencies as part of your request for funding. Many agencies have their own proposal request forms which you will need to follow. However, most require the following information:

### Introduction

Your introduction should include a brief description of who you are; what your aims and goals (short and long range) are; and why the particular agency you are addressing should be interested in funding your program.

### Program Design

The most important part of your proposal is the design of your program. Describe it accurately, especially how it will operate. The following topics should be covered explicitly.

### Day Care Facility

You should mention the date of your license to operate such a program, the number of children it will serve, and the adult-child ratio you plan.

### Environmental Standards

Among the most important of your selling points should be a complete description of your site (its location, composition, and so forth). Be sure to describe how your center will satisfy the requirements of all rules and regulations. You should stress how your site is especially suitable, providing all necessary day-care services.

### Educational Services

To show that you plan to provide learning experiences for children rather than mere custodial baby-sitting, you will need to describe your educational component in detail. A description should include a summary of your basic program goals; a description of staff responsible for implementing these goals; the procedures by which they will be achieved; and a brief description of the kinds of supplies, materials, and equipment you plan to use.

### Associated Services

All auxiliary components (nutrition, social service, health, psychological services) need to be explained in their relationship to the educational services which you have already described.

### Administration and Coordination
Describe the various administrative functions carried out in your program, and how responsibility for each area is allocated.

### Parent Involvement
Parent participation is important for ensuring continuity of care for children. Opportunities for involvement of parents in the center should be explained and specific parent participation described. Such a résumé might include a description of advisory committees, classroom parent representatives, parent meetings, parent-teacher meetings, and parent participation in classrooms.

### Staff Development
Your own plan for ensuring staff development through in-service, on-the-job, or some other method of training should be described.

### Evaluation
A final explanation of how you plan to ensure the quality of your program should be included in your proposal. Such a description might include teacher evaluations; child progress reports; testing results; and quarterly and annual reports.

### Budget
The actual cost of your program should be presented. Break down costs into appropriate areas, such as staff salaries; fringe benefits and administrative costs; equipment and supplies; food-service expenditures; travel allowances; space costs; utilities; and miscellaneous costs.

### Budget Justification
In order to prove that your budget is reasonable and worth funding, you will have to justify your costs. Under "staff" you should provide a brief summary of duties and explain why your particular staff members are qualified to perform the functions

described and why they should be paid the salaries you have requested. Actual fringe benefits should be specified and administrative costs defined.

A general justification in the categories of equipment, materials, and supplies should be supplemented by an appendix with each item listed with its price.

Food-service costs may be specified in general terms, but actual cost expenditures should be included in the form of an appendix.

Travel expenses for both children and staff will need to be justified also, as will your actual space and utility costs. Finally, the means by which you have estimated miscellaneous expenses should be explained.

### SUMMARY

In this chapter we have attempted to acquaint you with the various means of funding your day-care program; describe in detail how you might plan an operating budget; and finally, explain how you should prepare a proposal requesting funds to operate your center. While the actual cost of your program will be determined by many factors, some of which may be unique or common only to your geographic area, our discussion has attempted to provide you with a universal framework for budget planning and program funding. It should be apparent, as we have stressed again and again, that only you can make the final decisions for your own infant day care center. Our recommendations should be taken only as general suggestions rather than as a model to be copied exactly.

CHAPTER SIX

# Locating Your Center

When you are familiar with your state's rules and regulations for infant day care, have defined the scope and size of your proposed program, and have secured adequate funding for program development, you will need to complete arrangements for establishing your center.

As mentioned in chapter 5, "Preparing a Budget and Raising Funds," you must procure your initial capital. Once these funds have been found, it is imperative that you make a preliminary survey of several possible site locations. You can make the final selection on the basis of how much money you have. You may have adequate funds, so that you can purchase or rent what you believe is the ideal location. On the other hand, you may be forced to settle for a second or even a third choice. In this chapter we will furnish you with a measuring stick to evaluate possible sites.

## SELECTION CRITERIA

Since it is quite unlikely that you will ever find a perfect site (unless you have raised the money to construct it), we recommend you keep the following selection variables in mind in the order of priority listed below.

1. Your ideal potential site should have building construction of a kind and quality necessary to meet licensing standards. In many states this means brick, concrete, or stone construction, and first floor occupancy.
2. The building should provide at least the minimum square foot per child allowance required. (See chapter 4, "Licensing Requirements.")

3. The building should have adequate heating, plumbing, and electrical systems.

4. The interior space should be subdivided appropriately into usable classroom, kitchen, toilet, office, and other areas.

5. The exterior space is or can be fenced into an outdoor area which meets the minimum square-feet-per-child allowance required. (See chapter 4, "Licensing Requirements.")

6. The location is readily accessible to the community it serves, convenient to public transportation, and has adequate parking facilities.

Renovation costs are the key variable in selecting a site for your center. When looking at a prospective location, start at the top of the priority list and work your way down. If you get through No. 4, the chances are that the site holds good potential for development into a day care center.

The higher on the list are the criteria to which your potential site fails to conform, the more expensive your renovation costs will be.

Since diapering and toileting are especially important for this young age group, probably some plumbing renovations are unavoidable. And ready access to a well-equipped kitchen is necessary to facilitate individual infant feeding schedules.

Once these selection criteria are firmly fixed in your mind, you are ready to begin looking for a suitable location for your center.

SITE LOCATION

Each city, town, or region has a housing or building authority. This agency is responsible for maintaining lists of buildings available for purchase or rent, as well as for giving hints on soon-to-be-vacated sites. Real estate agents have listings of apartment or building vacancies also. If you explain your needs, they can be of tremendous assistance. You might also drive or walk through the area where you wish to locate your day care center. When you discover a potentially good site, check back with the housing authority to find out whether or not it is, or might be, available within a short time.

The ideal location for a day care center is a one-story building especially designed for children, with an adjoining outdoor play area. If you have money to build your own center, then you can design your site to fit your program needs. There are numerous examples of such buildings designed for specific programs; among them are American Child Centers, Inc. of Nashville, Tennessee; the primary division of Casady School, Oklahoma City; The Early Learning Center in Stamford, Connecticut; the Harold E. Jones Early Education Center in Berkeley, California; The Lamplighter School in Dallas, Texas; and the Phoebe Hearst Pre-School Learning Center in San Francisco.

A convenient yardstick to evaluate new construction costs is that most new buildings will range between a low of $14 per square foot to well over $25 per square foot.

Since only a few infant day-care organizers will be able to build a brand-new center, we believe we should include alternative suggestions. One of the best locations for a day care center is a one-family house. It has existing toilet and kitchen facilities, and usually an outdoor play area. With minor renovations, many private homes can be converted into warm, comfortable day care centers providing a homelike atmosphere which children will appreciate. Examples of day care centers now in operation located in former one-family dwellings are the Central Plaza Day School in St. Petersburg, Florida; the Child Minders School in Greenwich, Connecticut; and the New Nursery in Greeley, Colorado.

Private homes are not the only buildings suitable for conversion into day care centers. Our first day care center at Castle Square opened in a simple storefront in Boston. Fortunately, renovation costs were minimal since heating, lighting, and plumbing facilities were all in good condition. Further examples of successful conversion of a store into a day care center can be seen at the Hilltop Center in Dorchester, Massachusetts, and at Sea Pines Montessori School on Hilton Head Island, South Carolina.

Sometimes space for a day care center can be found in an old brick school building no longer in use because of population shifts or other reasons. While these buildings may appear shabby on first inspection, they are usually structurally sound, since they were originally built with the safety of children in mind. Unless the heating, wiring, and plumbing systems need to be replaced completely, old schools can be converted fairly inexpensively into excellent day care centers. The Kemper School and Strawberry Cottage in Arlington, Virginia, are two outstanding examples of old school buildings remodeled for modern day care use.

If single-unit locations are unobtainable, separate quarters may be found in some other type of building such as churches, public schools, apartments, and community centers. Sometimes you will discover that day care centers located within larger building units enjoy lower maintenance costs, and have the added advantage of being within walking distance of children's homes. One possible drawback may be high renovation costs. However, the fact remains that many community day care centers are established within larger building units.

Sometimes adequate space can be found in a local church. Our second day care center at Hawthorne House in Roxbury, Massachusetts, was established in a former convent. Since the area used for day care was formerly an orphanage, the plumbing, lighting, and heating facilities were adequate for our children. When we first viewed the site it seemed rundown—shabby, windows broken, walls in need of paint. However, since the building was structurally sound, the costs of renovation have been minimal.

Sometimes empty apartments can be found within a housing complex. Although plumbing and kitchen facilities will be available, usually walls must be removed to make workable classrooms. If you must locate your day care center in such a complex, try to get a ground-level apartment situated at an end of the building and near an outside entrance easily accessible for children. The infant center in the Bromley Heath Housing Project in Jamaica Plain, Massachusetts, is an example of one such site.

Additional site possibilities can be found within settlement houses, community centers, and the local YMCA and YWCA.

Sometimes desirable sites may be found outside the children's immediate neighborhood. For example, a day care center might be established in a complex where parents are employed. If the building is a hospital, factory, or large industrial complex, there are additional benefits. Parents could spend their lunch hours with their children. It may be possible to share medical personnel and other auxiliary services. Often these services are donated to the day care center by the larger organization, or can be purchased at nominal cost. In addition, such organizations are sometimes willing to donate space for day care or, at worst, charge only a minimal rent.

Since World War II, industries, mills, and factories have been intermittently receptive to the idea of day care centers. We feel strongly that day-care enrollment at such centers should include not only employees' children but also the children of residents of the community. This combination has been proved successful both at the KLH Child Development in Cambridge, Massachusetts, and at the AVCO Corporation (Crispus Attucks) Day Care Center in Dorchester, Massachusetts.

A recent Women's Bureau Survey entitled *Day Care Services: Industry's Involvement* (Bulletin 296, 1971) describes several day care centers operated by textile companies (Curlee Clothing, Mr. Apparel, Skyland Textile, Tioga Sportswear, and Vanderbilt Shirt); food-processing companies (Tyson Foods and Winter Garden Freezing Co.); and electronic firms (Arco Economic Systems, Control Data Corporation, and Bro-Dart Industries). In all these centers, children are cared for in facilities located within, adjacent to, or adjoining company property. Some centers were built by the companies, but the majority were converted from homes, warehouses, or other types of available space. Most of these industry-based centers are of medium size, each serving approximately forty to sixty-five children.

The Amalgamated Clothing Workers of America has helped sponsor five day care centers which together care for almost one thousand children of union working mothers. Four centers are sponsored by the Baltimore Regional Joint Board and are located in Baltimore, Maryland; Chambersburg and Hanover, Pennsylvania; and Verona, Virginia. The other center is operated by the Chicago Joint Board.

Another union, The United Federation of Teachers, has contracted with the New York City Board of Education for an early-childhood program integrating the children of teachers working in poverty-area schools with the children of local residents.

Three federal departments have established day care centers for employees. One is operated by The National Capital Area Day Care Association for sixty children of Department of Labor employees. The ages of the children range from nineteen months to five years. Another center has been set up in Beltsville, Maryland, by employees of the Agriculture Department Research Center. A third has been developed by the Department of Health, Education, and Welfare.

Many hospitals are becoming interested in providing day-care services as a means of attracting employees. Another Women's Bureau Publication, *Child Care Services Provided by Hospitals* (Bulletin 295, 1970), states that ninety-eight hospitals in thirty-five states are operating child-care centers for use of their personnel. These centers provided services to 3,700 children. The center at the Lemuel Shattuck Hospital in Jamaica Plain, Massachusetts, enrolls both the children of employees and children living in the area.

Recently colleges and universities have become interested in day care, providing space on campus for centers. Brandeis University, in Waltham, Massachusetts; Harvard University; and Tufts University, in Medford, Massachusetts, are three examples of this trend.

In the light of these new developments, you should not ignore the possibility of stimulating an interest in day care at any nearby industry, hospital, college or university, shopping center, or other large business complex.

## LEGAL REQUIREMENTS

As soon as you have selected a site for your center you will need to obtain a license. Call or write the licensing agency in your state (see Appendices, pages 144–145), and ask for an application for a license to operate an infant day-care unit.

Although one public agency is usually responsible for establishing regulations, issuing licenses, and the continuing supervision of programs, you may need to get site approval from other state and/or local agencies such as the following.

### Building Inspector
Local and/or state building department approval may be required. Inspections usually cover electrical wiring, plumbing, health and safety, and general building construction.

### Department of Sanitation

In many states sanitary inspectors are required to approve and to inspect periodically all toilet and kitchen facilities of agencies serving the public.

### Fire and Safety Marshals

Fire department approval may be required to ensure that fire and safety regulations are maintained. General requirements may include ground-level space, fire alarm systems, adequate sprinkler systems and/or fire extinguishers, heavy insulation, and at least two exits from all rooms used by children. Moreover, some communities will not allow day-care programs to operate in wood frame buildings.

### Zoning Commission

Housing for the day care center must conform to state and local zoning regulations. Sometimes a special exception, called a "variance," may be obtained by vote of a council or board of appeals after a public hearing.

Thus, once you have discovered who licenses day care in your area, you must ascertain what is actually regulated by this agency or agencies. The specific environmental standards required for the operation of day care centers vary from state to state, as does enforcement of these regulations.

Yielding to the increased pressure for day-care services, many states are currently revising rules and regulations. The old regulations were based on hospital and restaurant licensing requirements, and have demonstrated little value when transferred as standards regulating day-care services. Therefore do not become too overwhelmed by the seemingly endless list of present environmental requirements. Many of these rulings are being changed, and sometimes are being overlooked or "waived." Moreover, most inspectors recognize how difficult it is to comply with regulations in all respects.

CHAPTER SEVEN

# Developing Your Center

While the actual organization of space within your center will depend on many different limiting factors (including size, room arrangement, plumbing, electrical sources, and kitchen location), there are several areas where you can be creative, while at the same time providing the requisites for all programs that care for young children. In this chapter we describe the permanent aspects of the physical environment which you need to develop in order to care adequately for infants. Specific classroom design and curriculum materials will be discussed in chapter 9, "Developing the Classrooms for Infant-Toddlers and Toddler Two-Year-Olds."

## INDOOR ENVIRONMENT

### CLASSROOM AREA

There are several important environmental factors you must consider when establishing a center for young children.

*Space*
Young children need ample room to explore their physical environment and at the same time learn how to coordinate their bodies. Adequate space (no less than thirty-five square feet per child) is very important if each child is to learn how to crawl, climb, walk, and run.

*Lighting*
There should be both natural and artificial lighting in every classroom. Good lighting without glare is important in prevent-

ing eye fatigue, eyestrain, and even serious damage to the eyes. And children should have the opportunity to look through windows at the world outside.

### Heating

Young children spend much of their time crawling or sitting on the floor. It's extremely important that all drafts be eliminated and adequate heat reaches the floor area. Baseboard heating is perhaps best.

### Floor Surfaces

When considering various floor surfaces, you should keep in mind several factors: comfort, durability, resilience, maintenance costs, and acoustical control. At Castle Square we have found it most satisfactory to cover one-half of the infant classroom floor with linoleum and the other half with indoor-outdoor carpeting. Light-colored linoleum, asphalt, or vinyl tile are all easy to clean, and provide a perfect surface on which children may ride tricycles and kiddie cars, or use trucks, cars, and pull toys. The carpeted area is comfortable and safe for our crawling babies and young toddlers. Moreover, it's effective in softening noise, an important consideration.

### Acoustic Control

An infant center filled with happy exuberant children is a heartwarming sight. However, you should try to control excessive noise which can cause overstimulation, irritability, strain, and distraction. As mentioned, rugs help to absorb sound; so do draperies, soft easy chairs, and large floor pillows. Walls and ceilings should be covered with sound-absorbing materials also.

### Walls and Ceilings

In addition to absorbing sounds, walls and ceilings perform other functions. If painted white, or other light shades, they reflect light and provide a soft background for displaying children's vivid art and craftwork. Children's mobiles hung from the ceiling and artwork displayed at the child's height on bulletin boards and walls help provide a pleasant, interesting classroom for children and adults alike.

## CARETAKING FACILITIES

Essential elements of any preschool program include the caretaking aspects of eating, sleeping, and toileting. While these activities may seem routine to adults, they can provide a rich learning experience for children. Since a child's world is essentially egocentric, composed mainly of activities and feelings directly pertaining to himself, the basic functions of eating, sleeping, and elimination are especially significant.

### Eating

Eating is important not only for maintaining life but also for the developing emotions and behavior patterns. In fact, the infant's earliest feelings of comfort or discomfort, trust or mistrust, are concentrated mainly on satisfying his hunger. As he grows older, the child's appetite and behavior at mealtimes are sensitive indicators revealing his inner feelings. Therefore, it is important to provide a pleasant environment for eating, not only to ensure adequate nutrition but also to encourage personality development.

Because of the individual nature of infant feeding schedules, you'll need ready access to a kitchen. A small efficiency unit should contain at least a sink, refrigerator, stove, dishwasher, and cabinets for storage. At Castle Square we have built such a unit into the classroom alcove where the older infants and toddlers eat. Here teachers prepare cereal and baby food, and warm bottles. While research has demonstrated no ill effects caused by feeding infants cold milk, our teachers (all mothers themselves) feel strongly against it.

Even if you have an adequate kitchen for formula preparation, we advise you to use prepared formulas for your infants. While the initial cost may seem higher, actually you save both the teachers' time and effort and reduce the hazards of possible infection. A dishwasher should be used to wash and sterilize all bottles, dishes, and eating utensils used by infants.

All very young infants should be held while being fed. At Castle Square, as soon as infants are able to sit up we place them in individual chair-feeding tables in the kitchen area with young toddlers. Infants are allowed to experiment with finger-feeding by themselves and with assistance from teachers. Older toddlers sit on child-sized chairs at child-sized tables, using child-sized eating utensils. They feed themselves without assistance.

The small kitchen area is covered with linoleum for easy cleaning. While walls are brightly colored, there are no toys in sight to distract children while eating.

Plastic smocks are hung on individual hooks, and each child wears a smock while eating. Each child's own facecloth is hung nearby for washing face and hands before and after meals.

In our opinion, programs caring for very young infants need access to a small kitchen area. Here food can be prepared according to individual infant feeding schedules. Older infants and toddlers can eat in the kitchen area away from the distraction of toys and other stimuli. Food for older infants can be prepared in this small kitchen, or if your infant center is part of a larger day-care unit, it can be sent from the main kitchen and served in the smaller kitchen area.

Older toddlers and two-year-olds don't need such an expensive setup in their classrooms. However, a small refrigerator does come in handy for storing milk and juice because some children may like to take a bottle to bed with them at naptime.

Ensuring a positive, accepting attitude toward eating is one of the most important goals to be stressed at the day care center. At mealtime a child is introduced to a variety of nutritionally desirable foods and encouraged to practice accepted customs regarding eating, whatever they may be. The following are general suggestions about eating at the day care center:

Child-sized tables, chairs, and eating utensils should be used; children will enjoy eating more if they are comfortable and can manage the implements. If tables have been used for other activities, they must be cleared and cleaned. Often children enjoy helping clean and set up tables in anticipation of mealtime. While picnics and eating out of doors provide enjoyable variation occasionally, most meals should be served while children are sitting comfortably around a table in their classroom or lunchroom area.

Be sure tables are set and food is ready to serve before children are allowed to sit down. A group of young children just sitting, waiting, become restless very quickly. In many programs, children help clean up the room, wash their hands, and then enjoy a quiet group activity such as a story prior to eating. This helps calm children down after active play, so they will enjoy their food and table conversation.

If possible, there should be at least one adult per table, not only to supervise but also to provide a role model. Children learn through imitation; therefore, an adult who enjoys a wide variety of different foods, enjoys eating, and uses appropriate table manners can do much to teach children about food and table manners directly and by example.

Servings to young children should be small. The amount of food different children will eat varies, as does the amount of food the same child will eat at different times. If first servings are small, then a hungry child can ask for seconds, while the child with a small appetite will not be overwhelmed by what seems like a vast amount of food.

For young children, family-style serving, where the teacher serves the meal to each child, or where the child helps himself, is preferable to standard cafeteria service. Not only is the amount served more likely to be in accordance with the child's needs, but family-style service is more homelike and encourages conversation.

Most preschool children enjoy simple foods that "look good," contrast in color, and are served attractively.

Children should never be deprived of food as punishment for unacceptable behavior occurring at other times during the day. This punitive action can only be seen as unfair, since the punishment is in no way connected with the misbehavior. It can only create hostility and resentment in the child.

Encouraging children to assist with cleaning up helps them develop a sense of logical sequence and achieve a feeling of completeness.

Most states have rules and regulations governing food preparation and feeding. Be sure to check the requirements in your state. Additional information about nutrition and food service can be found on pages 130–134.

*Sleeping*

You will need a separate area away from the busy, noisy classroom where babies can nap according to their individual schedules. Such a crib room should be used only for *sleeping* infants. At Castle Square we put a large window between the classroom and sleeping room, so infants can be observed easily while napping without being disturbed.

Each crib should have a mobile over it for babies to look at when they awaken. We feel strongly that infants should not remain in their cribs when wide awake, but should join the other children in the classroom.

Ideally, there should be a diapering area in the crib room, so infants can be changed before and after napping. Since cribs take up an enormous amount of room, children should begin to sleep on cots as soon as possible. We try to have toddlers nap on cots as soon as they begin to walk. It not only saves space, since cots can be stored when not in use, but also eliminates the danger of children climbing out of cribs and getting hurt.

While very young infants sleep according to their own individual schedules, we recommend that you try to get older infants and young toddlers onto a regular morning and afternoon nap routine. In the infant center at Castle Square, children are encouraged to take a short rest after juice at 10:00 A.M. and a longer nap in the afternoon, from 2:00 P.M. to 3:00 P.M.

Our older toddlers and two-year-olds require only one long afternoon nap after lunch, sleeping on their own cots in the classroom. After naptime, cots are stacked and stored out of the way.

Naptime is something most preschool children require but often resist. Often children find it difficult to leave an exciting, stimulating environment to rest quietly and even sleep. The teacher must feel confident that a nap period is good for children if she expects to convince them to cooperate. Moreover, she must be able to communicate her convictions to them.

Maintaining limits regarding naptime behavior is often difficult for children because of their greater dependency needs at this time, and conversely their need to rebel against adult-imposed demands.

The way a teacher maintains limits at naptime may support and reassure a child or undermine his sense of self. By quietly whispering a reminder of her expectation, and reassuring him with a smile and a comforting pat, the teacher is often able to help a child settle down to rest. Disapproving frowns and threats may mean to the child general disapproval of him as a person. By making a child feel uncomfortable and/or angry, the teacher may inadvertently be encouraging resistance and rebellion at naptime, sometimes leading to a vicious cycle of revolt and consequent reprisal.

Often such confrontations can be prevented by creating an atmosphere that suggests rest. Several suggestions may help to make naptime more pleasant.

Young children like the security of routine, so naptime will be more successful if it occurs at the same time every day. Most centers find that children are ready for sleep immediately after the noonday meal.

Each child should have his own cot and blanket clearly marked with his name. Not only is this good health practice, but labeling gives the child a sense of identity and reinforces the expectations of naptime.

Cots should be put in the same place for nap period each day, so the child knows where he belongs. There should be adequate space between cots (at least two feet) to allow good ventilation and prevent children from disturbing each other. Children who have trouble resting should not be placed beside one another. When possible, a separate room should be used for those children who have difficulty sleeping or are apt to bother others.

Often a darkened, quiet room assists children in sleeping. Usually preschool children require no more than an hour or two of rest. A child who continually sleeps longer than two hours, or falls asleep consistently at other times during the day, should be referred for medical and social follow-up.

There should be a regular procedure for ending naptime. In some centers, as children waken they are assisted in putting their cots and blankets away, and directed toward a quiet activity. When most children are awake, or enough are ready to join in small-group activity, one or more teachers will take the group out of doors or to another area in the center. At least one teacher must remain with the sleeping children at all times to insure safety, and assist them as they waken.

Children in an all-day program need a regular rest time daily. Teachers can help children gain the relaxation and sleep they need through supportive reassurance and patient understanding. The teacher should not attempt to force a child to sleep, but she should expect him to respect the sleep rights of other children.

### Diapering and Toileting

Almost all infants under the age of two, and many children under three may require diapering. To provide proper care, you should have adequate diaper-change areas. As mentioned previously, we suggest one such area be located, if possible, in the crib room to facilitate diapering before and after naps. In addition to a waist-high counter surface on which to lay the baby, the diapering area should contain a large sink with hot and cold running water for bathing children, if necessary, and for washing off babies with each diaper change. Children should be washed with *every* change of diapers, as urine contains ammonia, which rapidly breaks down a baby's skin if care is not taken. Every child should have a special washcloth used only for this purpose and laundered daily. Furthermore, a coating of Vaseline, Desitin, or baby lotion should be applied to babies' bottoms at each change to provide a protective layer between skin and excrement.

While a change area is helpful in a crib room, the main change counter should be located within the larger classroom area, where teachers can change diapers without disturbing sleeping babies, at the same time supervising other children in the classroom.

In the case of older toddlers and two-year-olds, it's helpful to have the diapering area adjacent to the bathroom. This will help children understand the connection between elimination and toileting activities, and ease the transition from diapers to toilet training. As in the infant center, all children in diapers need to be washed, using their own cloths exclusively for this purpose. Again, these cloths require daily washing.

Toileting is a significant experience in the life of a young child for many reasons. The circumstances surrounding his toilet training may be conducive to promoting feelings of self-confidence and self-esteem or failure and inadequacy. Either outcome affects many aspects of behavior. Often excessive negativism derives from rigid early toilet training procedures. Various inhibitions which may affect spontaneity and creativity can also be traced to the same source. Loss of self-confidence is a further result of overly strict toilet training.

Fortunately many children are allowed to become toilet trained at their own rate as they develop physical and emotional maturity. These children are rewarded for their successes rather than penalized for their failures.

What are some constructive procedures regarding toileting practices at the day care center?

The physical setup plays an important role in helping build a child's positive feelings toward toileting. The room itself should be pleasant, well lighted, and attractive. Furthermore, the surroundings should help the child feel safe and comfortable. Heavy doors which shut children off from others during toileting can produce anxiety and fear. Any massive doors should be removed entirely or replaced with latticed or free-swinging booth doors. Separate toilet facilities for girls and boys are not necessary in preschool; the toileting arrangement should be casual and matter-of-fact at this age.

If children are to learn to care for themselves, they need equipment well suited for their use. Many children are afraid of falling into an adult-sized toilet; child-sized toilets are preferable. If such equipment is too expensive, a special seat can be constructed to make the opening smaller.

When converting adult-sized toilets for children's use, you should also make a step platform in front of the toilet to provide easy access. Moreover, children feel safer and more comfortable when they can rest both feet on a firm surface.

A sink should be located in or near the toileting area for handwashing and encouraging good hygiene habits. Children should be encouraged to wash their hands after toileting, and handwashing should be required before they are allowed to eat.

Lower the sinks to a height easily reached by young children, or construct step platforms so they can reach the basins without assistance. Hang a mirror securely over wash basins to help children see the results of their efforts.

Soap and paper towels should also be provided in the washroom, as well as a wastebasket for disposal of used towels. A word of caution! Paper-towel dispensers should be placed as far away from the toilets as possible. Children often enjoy stuffing paper down the toilet and then watching it flush away. Often paper towels clog the toilet drain.

In an all-day program it's necessary for each child to have his own washcloth and towel for more extensive cleaning. Each washcloth and towel should be clearly marked with the child's name and hung on separate assigned hooks placed so that neither cloths nor towels touch each other. All washcloths and towels should be laundered daily. Extra washcloths come in handy for cleaning children after "accidents."

Ideally each classroom should have its own toilet and washroom facilities. When toilets are located at a distance from classroom areas, adult assistance and supervision become increasingly difficult.

Since a set toileting schedule rarely meets individual needs, every attempt should be made to avoid such a pattern. However, most teachers find it advisable to suggest toileting for all children at intervals such as midmorning, lunchtime, and before and after nap.

Often problems concerning toilet training occur at a day care center because of training procedures begun at home. Since feelings and behavior are closely linked with toileting, a sensitive, understanding teacher can promote self-confidence and encourage independence. "Accidents" should be handled in matter-of-fact fashion, and every attempt should be made to discover the cause if these episodes are repeated. If teachers are relaxed and supportive of toileting procedures, children will feel more at ease and accept toilet training as a normal ordinary procedure.

### Laundry

It's very helpful to have a laundry area with a sink, washer, and dryer. If you plan to launder your own diapers, this equipment is a necessity. Even if you use disposable diapers (which we strongly recommend) you will have washcloths, towels, sheets, blankets, and clothing to launder each day. At Castle Square our washer and dryer are located next to the kitchen and within the confines of the infant center. Children often "help" teachers with laundry during the school day. After a busy morning of painting, pasting, or other messy art activities, toddlers' clothes need washing. Usually we find that babies require several changes of clothing a day. Therefore, all our children under one year are changed into colorful school jumpsuits when they arrive in the morning, so they may be changed as often as necessary and still have their own dry clothing to wear home. Toddlers and two-year-olds remain in their own clothing, and we ask parents to bring a change of clothes for use in case of "accidents." In addition, the school maintains a large supply of assorted clothing for emergency use.

Sometimes in midmorning, and always at the end of each day, all soiled clothing is washed, dried, and put away for use the next day.

### Office

In addition to child classrooms you will need office space for your administrative staff. The size will be determined by the needs of your program.

### Isolation

A small room should be available at the center to isolate any child suspected of being infected with a contagious disease. A teacher or some other staff member should remain with the sick child until he is picked up by his parents.

If you have sufficient funds, you might consider having a small sick bay, staffed by a nurse at your center, for children who are recovering from minor illnesses and need extra care and rest before they join the larger group. Under no circumstances should you attempt to care for very ill children, or children with contagious communicable diseases such as measles, chicken pox, mumps, and scarlet fever.

### Observation

Unless you want visitors to come directly into your classroom (and we don't think this is a good idea for infants and very young children), you must design an area where they will be out of the way, but still able to observe the children. The simplest method is to cut a window either in a door or wall of the classroom and cover it with a two-way mirror or double-mesh screening. At Castle Square we have constructed observation booths four feet off the floor, each holding between eight and ten people. Originally we had large booths for twenty adults, but we found observers were so rude and distracting to the children (waving, talking loudly, smoking, eating, laughing) that we were forced to either supervise the booths constantly or ask adults to leave. Since no one had time for "policing," we were forced to cut down the size of the booths, so adult observers would behave themselves.

Our children are accustomed to visitors. Usually they ignore them unless distracted by them. We use double screening in our booths rather than two-way mirrors, for several reasons. First, we feel it is more honest. Children soon discover what two-way glass is and waste much time cupping their hands over the glass, so they can peer back at observers. Secondly, large mirror areas are very distracting. Finally, the microphone system enabling observers to hear children is both cumbersome and very expensive.

### Storage

A final item you need to consider when developing your indoor environment is adequate storage space. We found that storage space within the classroom is necessary, as well as a central depot for supplies and materials purchased in bulk, such as paint and paper. Within the classroom, all materials and supplies children are not supposed to handle must be stored safely out of reach.

If you have elevated observation booths, the space underneath is excellent for storing cots, tricycles, and other large equipment.

## OUTDOOR ENVIRONMENT

In many European countries infants are taken out of doors every day. If you don't have an outdoor area, you can take babies for rides in carriages and strollers. Older infants and toddlers enjoy excursions to nearby parks, fields, and similar recreation areas, but these trips cannot substitute for an outdoor area of their own. Young active preschool children like an exciting outdoor environment with many opportunities for creating, exploring, discovering, and learning. They need opportunities to make an impact on their environment, invent and improvise, build and destroy, to make things work and learn how and why. Such an environment should be considered an integral part of the education process.

### MATERIALS AND EQUIPMENT

Children don't need elaborate, expensive equipment to enjoy and profit from an outdoor area. All the needs mentioned earlier can be met by sensitive adults who provide children with the basic raw materials for learning outdoors.

#### Sand

Sand is one of the basic materials children enjoy most because it is malleable. By using only his hands, a child can dig, pile, sift, build, tunnel, mold, and design creatively. An outdoor area should have a large sandbox (at least 100 square feet). Any assortment of inexpensive implements (spoons, cups, cans, sifters, scoops, shovels, bowls, pans, molds, and so forth) may be used with sand, giving children many hours of pleasurable learning activity. Often it is wise to shade the sandbox area with an awning if your site is not protected by shade trees.

#### Water

Water is probably the most popular of all natural play materials for young children. It fascinates them. They enjoy exploring its many properties. Water can be poured, squirted, slapped, sprayed, and splashed. Toys can be floated, sunk, whirled, or dropped in water, each action producing different results. Children should be encouraged to explore water. Fill tubs, plastic pools, or water tables and give children a wide variety of inexpensive water-play equipment: clear plastic bottles; syringes (naturally without needles); watering cans; assorted lengths and diameters of plastic tubing; short lengths of garden hose; a variety of brushes (scrubbing, wallpaper, and smaller one-inch and two-inch for "painting" with water); soap for making bubbles and washing doll clothes; food coloring to color water; toys and materials which will sink or float; cups, spoons, cans, and other containers for pouring; cork, wood, metal—all for experimenting with water.

### Dirt

The outdoor space should have grassy areas, shrubs, plants, and trees. In addition, provide an open space for digging and another for gardening. Here children can explore the most basic natural materials of life, and by tending their garden watch one of life's greatest mysteries unfold. Too often, adults forget the wonders of nature, and how important it is for a child to experiment; for life attracts life—living plants bring bees, butterflies, and other insects, all fascinating objects for study. Rakes, hoes, shovels, trowels, watering cans, garden hose, wheelbarrow, and other equipment will help children care for their plants and flowers, and experiment with earth and mud.

### Building Materials

Children are doers; they love to create, dismantle, and rebuild anew. Simple materials such as odd lengths of wood, boards, barrels, hollow blocks, cartons, large spools, packing crates, boxes, sticks, pieces of metal, stones, string, old tires, rope, and cloth can be used by children to create new and exciting worlds in dramatic play.

### Climbing Structures

Healthy children have strong needs for release of tension, mobility, and noisy, dramatic action. The outdoor area is especially well suited to provide for these needs. Children enjoy climbing many different structures, especially those they construct themselves. Large packing crates, ladders, and sturdy planks are excellent for this purpose. And, they offer a wider variety of experiences than a sterile jungle gym. Children can create new structures geared to their interests and abilities when given the proper tools.

If permanent structures are imposed on an area they should be portable, readily adapted to children's changing purposes. For example, you might construct an outdoor house with stairways, outside ladders of both wood and rope, wide rope mesh for climbing, and different platforms and floor levels. You might also add an extension arm to the playhouse and hang swings from it. Children could use the building as a house, fort, castle, or store for dramatic play, and the structure would provide much physical exercise, too.

A large mound of dirt or a grassy hill is excellent for climbing, running, and rolling down. You might also make a tunnel through the hill with a large sewer pipe, and build a sliding area down one slope.

### Wheeled Vehicles

Part of the outdoor area should be paved. If a ten-foot-wide space next to the building is paved with concrete or asphalt, then partially roofed over, you will have year-round protection against too much sun, rain, or snow. This area may be used in weather conditions that make the rest of the playground unusable. A paved, winding walk or roadway starting at this point and curving through the rest of the play yard affords variety and lessens traffic congestion. The roadway should be wide enough to allow tricycles, doll carriages, carts, wagons, wheelbarrows, trucks, and pedal cars to pass each other.

### Other Outdoor Activities

Weather permitting, almost every activity which takes place inside the classroom can be done just as effectively outside. Children can listen to stories read to them in the shade of an awning or, preferably, a shade tree, or be free to choose picturebooks to examine on their own.

Art can be enjoyed out of doors. Often children feel freer, less inhibited when experimenting with art materials outside. Painting need not be confined to paper. Painting on windows can be fun too. "Painting" with water is another exciting experience.

Woodworking can be extended easily to outdoor construction, while applied science and mathematics are naturals out of doors.

Finally, music, creative movement, singing, and dancing are particularly satisfying outside where the sun, large expanses of space, and little prohibition on noise allow for greater freedom of creative expression.

### Storage

Proper storage space is required to protect materials and equipment. Often you can attach a storage shed to the playhouse or the main building. A suggested size is 10 by 12 feet with a 7-foot ceiling. Doors should open wide enough to admit large wheeled toys easily. Inside, painted lines can designate parking spaces for wheeled vehicles. In addition, shelving 2 or 3 feet wide will store such items as boards, outdoor hollow blocks, portable ladders, baskets for water and sand-play toys, and balls. Underneath the shelves, you should construct bins for assorted "junk" materials—ropes, hoops, pieces of wood, and cloth. Snap hooks on the opposite wall allow orderly storage of garden tools.

### SIZE, SAFETY, SUPERVISION

Although we have described the components of a quality outdoor space, up to this point we have ignored questions about size, safety, and supervision. Many states mandate a minimum of 75 square feet of outdoor space per child. In our opinion this requirement represents the barest minimum for functional use. At least 100 square feet per child is necessary. However, the actual amount of space is not nearly so important as its arrangement. The organization and wise management of available space provide the best solution for maximum use.

If children are to use the outdoor area freely, safety must be ensured. Enclosing the play yard with a 4- to 7-foot fence allows children to play safely; you won't have to worry if a child wanders while the others are engaged in some group activity. Enclosure makes adult supervision much easier. Obviously safety and responsible supervision must go hand in hand. We suggest you check carefully to see whether you have taken the following precautions:

Be sure that a soft landing surface (such as sand, dirt, or a rubber mat) is provided at the end of the slide. The safest slides are built into hills or mounds; a child cannot fall off the top or over the sides. Free-standing slides need fenced-in platforms at the top to prevent falls.

Place swings out of the paths of traffic (carts, carriages, and kiddie cars) and outside busy play areas. Plastic discs, rubber tires, canvas or leather seats are preferable to the conventional hard wooden or metal swings. Pedestrian toddlers may be hurt colliding with a swinger.

Hard surfacing, such as concrete or asphalt, should not be used beneath climbing structures. Grass, sand, or rubber surfacing helps prevent injuries from falls.

Keep all materials and equipment in good repair, free from splinters, jagged edges, or loose parts.

An outdoor play area, supervised responsibly by adults, gives children an exciting and stimulating environment. They may safely create and explore—experimenting with a variety of materials and assorted equipment, and experiencing a wide range of problem-solving and learning activities.

CHAPTER EIGHT

# Staffing Your Program

The key element in any infant day care center is the quality of people responsible for program operations and child care. No matter what the size of your center, there are several distinct functions which must be carried out by the staff. Among these are program direction, supervision, and actually providing daily child care. Whether the program divides these functions among a few individuals filling several roles, or assigns each person a different role, will depend on the size of the center and your resources. We shall discuss these functions separately, even though you may wish to combine one or more of these roles.

## PROGRAM DIRECTION AND SUPERVISION

Whether you are beginning a new center or adding an infant component to an existing center, someone must assume responsibility for program direction and staff supervision. In very small centers of less than twenty-four children a teacher-director may be able to handle both administrative and some teaching responsibilities. If there are more than twenty-four children, the director should not assume major teaching responsibilities or be counted in the staff:child ratio. In our opinion, a nonteaching director is needed in centers caring for more than forty children; the administrative role here is a full-time job.

Optimally, the director will be someone knowledgeable about children and their needs, as well as a competent administrator. While some people believe that (in large centers especially) the director need only be an executive, highly experienced in program administration, we feel strongly that a good director must be experienced in working with children, and able to work cooperatively with staff and parents.

Some states require that the director be a college graduate with a degree in early childhood education, or some related field. We support this requirement, especially for large centers, because professional leadership is necessary to ensure optimal program policy and staff supervision. We prefer that the director be expert in child care, while his/her assistant handles administrative tasks competently, rather than the reverse.

Among the director's most important responsibilities should be the following:

1. To formulate child-care policy decisions in conjunction with the governing board, staff, and parents.

2. To hire and fire staff as necessary. Many centers involve parents and other staff members in this process but the director should play a significant role in making these decisions.

3. To supervise and evaluate periodically the performance of all personnel at the center.

4. To conduct an in-service training program for staff development which includes, at minimum, regular staff meetings, periodic supervision, and learning-workshop sessions.

5. To secure adequate funding and adhere to budget limitations. Unless the center is financed completely by charitable organizations, or is a part of a public agency, the director will have to assume responsibility for funding the child-care program. Often this is a very time-consuming task requiring the piecing together of funds from various sources, such as parent fees, donations, and local charities. The director may also be required to write and submit proposals to both government and private foundations for additional grants. If the center is small, the director will need bookkeeping skills to keep track of funds received and paid. He/she will be responsible for ordering all supplies and equipment, and must adhere to budget limitations. Making out the payroll may become his/her responsibility if not delegated to a local bank or administrative assistant.

6. To recruit children according to the policy practices of the center may be part of his/her duties. In larger cen-

ters this function is usually delegated to the social worker or social service coordinator.

7. To maintain health and safety standards. Unless the center employs a nurse, the director must be sure that health records for both children and staff are up to date and a medical record for each is on file.

8. To make certain that children receive adequate nutrition, according to an approved infant feeding schedule. Unless a consultant nutritionist is available, the director must plan all menus for children eating solid foods, and secure a written formula prescription from each infant's physican if prepared formulas are not used.

9. To maintain good public relations with the community and assist others to learn more about day-care operations. Often such duties require that the director receive visitors at the center, as well as attend meetings and conferences outside.

10. To refer to other community services and agencies problems outside the scope of the center's activities. If the center does not have a consultant doctor, nurse, dentist, psychologist, and/or social worker, the director must help parents get whatever care is needed.

As you can see, the director is responsible for organizing and administering a wide range of functions. Only a very exceptional person can handle all jobs equally well, and if the center is large, even a very competent person will not have time to fulfill all the responsibilities described above. In large centers, certain administrative tasks must be delegated to others, i.e., administrative assistant, bookkeeper, secretary-receptionist, social worker, nurse, doctor, dentist, and psychologist.

## DAILY CHILD CARE

Not everyone can work with young children. State rules and regulations, where they exist, are stated in such general terms, they are not very helpful in describing appropriate qualifications for teachers. It will depend on you, the organizer, to determine what kind of people you want to work with your children. Naturally your choice will be subjective, based on your

own personal value judgments regarding "good" teachers. It's
necessary to formulate in your mind, or preferably on paper,
the essential policy elements of your own program. How much
structure do you believe young children need in the classroom?
Should you have an "open" program or follow an infant curriculum? What routines, if any, do you feel are important? Answers
to these and other questions must be made by the person or
persons responsible for hiring. Most centers have a representative hiring board reflecting the values of parents, the governing
board, teaching staff, and program director.

Only you, the organizers, know what you want for your
children and the sort of persons you believe can perform best.
However, we shall suggest guidelines for selecting teachers
which you may find helpful. We arrived at our own definition
of a "good" teacher for children under three both by studying
relevant research and by trial-and-error experience employing
teachers in the Castle Square Infant Center.

## SUGGESTED QUALIFICATIONS

### Maturity
Maturity shouldn't be measured so much by years as by
experience with children and a sense of self-fulfillment. A mature teacher is able to meet the demands of very young children
because he/she has achieved a sense of identity and acceptance
of self. We've found some mature teachers in their early twenties, but our most successful teachers of very young children are
usually mothers between the ages of twenty-eight and forty.
Most adolescents are definitely *not able* to meet the insatiable
demands of young children on a full-time basis, since they need
time to solve their own problems of identity and ego development. They are helpful as volunteers and part-time assistants,
but should never be given full-time responsibility.

### Reliability
Most young children feel the need of consistency in a
stable adult-child relationship. While we don't assign a particular child to a certain teacher, children have a way of showing
their own preference. And teachers seem more at ease with
some children than with others. Insofar as possible, we allow
our staff and children to find each other and build a mutually

trusting relationship. It's very important that each child's "special" teacher be present every day. Occasionally illness may separate child and teacher, but exceptionally good attendance records are important for both children and their teachers to maintain a stable, consistent relationship.

### Responsibility

The responsibility of caring for another person's child is sometimes rewarding but always challenging. A teacher must protect children from harm in the parent's absence, and during those hours when a child is at the center, a teacher is responsible for all facets of his development, be it physical, mental, social, or psychological. We know how important the earliest formative years are in promoting optimal development.

### Stability

We feel children need to feel a sense of order, stability, and predictability in their world. A caretaker subject to erratic moods and irrational behavior does not help children plan or make predictions about their own actions, since the same action may produce various responses on different occasions. On the other hand, a stable adult, consistent in his/her handling and expectations, helps children understand their world and move more comfortably in it.

### Ability to Set and Maintain Reasonable Limits

A teacher of young children must set limits for them, maintain these limits consistently, and feel comfortable in imposing these restrictions on children's freedom. A permissive approach in handling very young children is not as appropriate as it may be later when the child has learned to discipline himself. We have learned through experience that the most successful teachers caring for our youngest children are those who are more conservative, more autocratic, more willing to make decisions for children than are permissive and more creative teachers (who work best with our children of three years and older). We believe it's inappropriate to attempt to require infants and toddlers to set their own limits. Not only are they incapable of doing so, but their attempts result in complete frustration. For example, a teacher who is hesitant about whether he should break up a fight conveys this insecurity to the children involved. Then the children test the teachers until they know where limits lie, how much responsibility they are expected to assume for their own behavior, and how much will be decided for them by adults. A word of caution—the staff should not be so authoritarian that they impose unreasonable restrictions on children, or so inflexible that they are not willing to modify restrictions as children develop self-discipline during the year.

### Cooperation

An ability to work closely with other teachers and parents is perhaps most essential in teaching younger groups. Routine questions, such as when a baby last ate, had a bowel movement, slept, assume great importance. Parents must feel free to tell teachers pertinent facts each day and, in turn, the staff must communicate with each other and with parents on a daily basis to ensure continuity of routine.

### Warmth

Very young children must feel loved. They need to be held, kissed, hugged, and rocked. Persons caring for young children must show their feelings for children in a warm, spontaneous manner.

### Energy

Needless to say, young children are extremely active, and adults working with them must be strong and energetic. Recently an experiment was conducted in which an athlete in top physical condition was required to follow a toddler around, imitating every motion and sound he made. By midmorning the athlete was exhausted, unable to continue with the experiment. The toddler continued tirelessly at his own pace until evening, still alert and full of vim and vigor. Finally, he was put to bed in spite of his outraged protests. While teachers need not be athletes, supervising active toddlers is a demanding, tiring job, and what toddler is not active? Staff caring for this age group must be able to move quickly to prevent accidents, and must have a deep reserve of energy to sustain them throughout their long day.

Among the many other personal qualities adults working with young children should have are sensitivity to children's needs, resourcefulness, respect for individual personalities and racial and cultural differences. The organizer of a day care center should decide which qualities he/she feels are most important, and select teachers on that basis.

In addition to personal qualities, educational qualifications and evidence of maturity should be considered. Most states do not require that day-care staff be certified teachers. Although we agree that a college degree is no guarantee of superior teaching performance, we feel adults working with young children do need knowledge of children above and beyond natural intuition. However, given natural teaching ability, education and experience can be acquired rapidly and should include the following:

A basic knowledge of child growth and development, i.e., how infants and young children grow, develop and learn

A practical knowledge of appropriate games, toys, and activities to promote learning and development at each level

An ability to employ those teaching techniques applicable to group activities

An awareness of and a willingness to respond to children's individual needs

## STAFF DUTIES

Having selected persons whom you would like to work with young children, the next decision is just what will they do? Small centers may require teachers to prepare food for the children. Even in large centers, teachers may be responsible for preparing infant formulas and special diets for older children not furnished by the regular kitchen staff. At Castle Square, teachers in our infant center work with the pediatrician, the nutritionist, and the infant's mother to devise a feeding schedule for each child. Prepared formula and baby foods are kept in the infant center kitchen, and teachers are responsible for feeding babies the required foods. Older infants and toddlers without special problems eat food from the central kitchen, prepared by our two cooks, according to the menu devised by the nutritionist.

Teachers in a small center may also be responsible for maintenance. However, it should be evident that whenever teachers are diverted from their primary responsibility—working with children—the quality of the program must suffer as a result.

### Head Teacher

We have found it helpful to have a head teacher in every classroom. The head teacher need not be a college graduate, but should have had previous experience working with young children. He or she should be able to make a realistic appraisal of each child's abilities and evaluate his progress. To operate effectively he/she needs a basic understanding of child growth and development. Some states require head teachers to take two or more formal courses in child growth and development. Be sure to check your state rules regarding staff qualifications before hiring your teaching staff. A head teacher's duties involve the following:

1. The planning and execution of daily activities for children in cooperation with the other classroom teachers

2. Assessing each child's individual needs and attempting to fulfill them insofar as possible, considering the resources available in the classroom, center, and community

3. Writing periodic evaluations of each child, assessing his/her needs and abilities and suggesting a plan to promote further growth and development (see Appendices, page 153, for a suggested form on Child Progress Reports)

4. Supervising and coordinating activities of all other adults in the room—teachers, students, and volunteers

5. After planning and consultation with his/her teaching staff, making final decisions regarding the amount, type, and arrangement of all materials and equipment to be used in program activities

6. Representing his/her classroom at staff meetings to share ideas, experiences, concerns, and problems

7. Working cooperatively with parents to establish a consensus of what should be expected of each child, and

encouraging communication with parents through regular parent-teacher classroom meetings and individual
parent conferences

### Assistant Teacher

All adults in the classroom are regarded as "teachers" by
children. Often assistant teachers are in charge of small groups
of children, and may assume responsibility for the entire group
in the absence of the head teacher. For this reason, you must
be sure your assistant teachers are qualified to perform the necessary child-care responsibilities without constant direction from
the head teacher.

Assistant teachers should be able to do the following:

Assist the head teacher in planning and carrying out class
activities

Work cooperatively with other adults in the room

Share pertinent information about the children and their
parents with the rest of the "team"

Assume responsibility for children in small groups, and for
the entire group whenever necessary

Attend parent and staff meetings

### Educational Supervisor

If you have a large center, and especially if your director is
not an early-childhood educator, you ought to consider employing an experienced professional to supervise teachers and help
them plan the child-care program in each classroom. In addition, the educational supervisor can conduct an in-service training program to promote staff development.

### Auxiliary Staff

Professionals, such as a doctor, nurse, dentist, social worker,
and psychologist, may or may not be employed at your center.
Each performs highly specialized functions children may need.
If your center is small or lacks the necessary funds for full-time,
part-time, or even consulting professionals, you can sometimes
find a dedicated individual, willing to volunteer his/her services to your center. Sometimes this care can be arranged at
nearby clinics or hospitals. All efforts should be made to help

parents give their children the necessary auxiliary care the child does not receive at home or at the day care center. A comprehensive description of such services can be found in chapter 10, "Associated Services."

### Kitchen and Maintenance Staff

Cooks and janitors should not only do their usual jobs, but should also like children. Since all adults are important to children, these individuals also play an important role in their relationship with the children.

### Volunteers

Many individuals—students, parents, older people—may volunteer to help at your center. Volunteers can assist your staff in many ways. They can help with children by giving individual attention to a child who needs it, serve as an extra pair of hands on field trips or with other special activities, such as parties or walks, and in general be of assistance to the regular teaching staff. Moreover, they can type, answer the phone, greet visitors, repair equipment, and make toys, dolls' clothing, and other items. Under no circumstances should you use volunteers in place of regular staff. Your staff is legally responsible for children enrolled at the center. It is a dereliction of responsibility to entrust such care to others.

In our opinion, all volunteers should be willing to contribute at least eight hours a week to the center. Children in day care must form many different relationships—with teachers, other children, and other adults at the center. To make these relationships truly helpful and meaningful, the adults must be consistent. Children become very confused when exposed to different adults who impinge upon their lives without forming any attachments on an individual basis. In short, volunteers can perform useful functions in a day care center if they are willing to spend enough time to form meaningful relationships with children, and are adequately supervised.

For a full discussion of staff development and teacher-training techniques, see chapter 8, "Teacher Training," in the earlier book *Day Care.**

* E. Belle Evans, Beth Shub, and Marlene Weinstein, *Day Care* (Boston: Beacon Press, 1971), pp. 67–89.

# CHAPTER NINE

# Developing the Classrooms for Infant-Toddlers and Toddler Two-Year-Olds

From the very earliest days of life, the infant begins to learn about his world. According to Erik Erikson, the infant discovers first whether his environment is one in which he feels comfortable and happy or just the reverse. Erikson calls this stage the "trust versus mistrust" phenomenon.

If an infant is fed when hungry, changed when he needs diapering, receives stimulation from seeing, hearing, touching, and tasting; interacts socially with others through smiles, hugs, kisses, and rocking, then he begins to realize that his world is a safe place, a world in which there is only temporary discomfort followed by relief—in short, a world he can trust.

Quality infant day care can supplement home care and help infants achieve this sense of trust. It's imperative that an infant feel secure, for trusting relationships form the basis of healthy personality development.

At about eighteen to twenty-four months children begin to assert themselves. This is a normal development Erikson calls "autonomy." At this stage the young child wants to "do things himself." He is venturesome to the point of recklessness. He needs firm limits, but loudly protests any and all restrictions on his freedom. His reaction to any restraint is an emphatic "NO!"

Such toddler two-year-olds need the guidance of firm but kindly, understanding adults. Teachers need to set and maintain safe limits to protect children from serious injury, but shouldn't be so restrictive that children don't have the opportunity to explore and even experience an occasional bump or two, while learning from their environment or from interaction with other children. At all ages, but particularly at the toddler two-year-old stage, children need to be rewarded for efforts to establish autonomy. They need to experience success, and teachers should help each child feel that he/she is worthwhile, that he/she is a competent person.

How can a teacher, or any adult, for that matter, help a child develop autonomy instead of self-doubt? In the first place, a teacher can plan the classroom environment so children can explore all areas freely. This requires that anything not for children's use be stored out of their sight and reach. It makes supervision easier, decreasing the number of times a teacher must say no to a child.

A second way a teacher can help a child gain autonomy is permit him/her some initiative and choice whenever appropriate. Often opposition to naptime can be lessened by allowing the child choice of one favorite toy to take to bed with him.

Of primary importance at this age is the need for a child to feel successful in toilet training. He/she should be rewarded for successes rather than punished for mistakes. Rigid toilet-training practices—attempting to force a child to conform through spanking, shaming, or punishing—undermine a child's sense of personal worth and may cause feelings of self-doubt which carry over into other areas, often seriously curtailing his development. (See pages 89–92 for helpful suggestions regarding toileting at the day care center.)

Children learn to believe in themselves through repeated experiences which prove they are competent; repeated failures produce self-doubt and undermine their entire personality. Therefore, an exciting, safe environment, reinforced by praise and reward from adults when a child explores, shows curiosity, and asks questions, helps to encourage a child to feel that learning is both exciting and satisfying. Obviously a child who loves to learn, and is confident that he can, is more likely to be successful, not only in school and in social adjustment, but also in adult life. The goal of infant day care should be to enhance this development.

While all experts agree on the importance of these first early years, there is some disagreement as to how children should be assigned to groups in day care to promote optimal development. In many foreign countries (France, Yugoslavia,

Russia), infants are segregated in groups narrowly defined by chronological age. Other countries (Sweden, Denmark) have found narrow chronological age groupings to be both inhibiting and lacking in stimulation. Instead they place infants in mixed-age groups with other children aged six to twenty-four months. At Castle Square we found the most appropriate age grouping for children in our infant center is approximately one to eighteen months, and that the "ideal" group size is twelve. Because at this age the rate of absenteeism averages 25 percent, we can enroll approximately sixteen children in the infant center and still have our ideal group of twelve children present every day.

Usually four or five toddlers assemble in a group and play together. Our middle infants (eight to twelve months) crawl on the floor and play with toys or scoot around the classroom in walkers, investigating and exploring, while our youngest babies play with their rattles, tray toys, and so forth, or examine mobiles and watch other children.

While chronological age can be used as a rough measuring stick, we do not use it as our primary index for grouping children. We found children are ready to be promoted into our toddler group when they can understand and comply with directions or when they display aggressive behavior toward younger infants by biting, hitting, or pulling hair. When they can understand and follow directions, toddlers are ready for larger group activities. In like manner, when aggressive infants are placed with children their own age or slightly older they are much more reluctant to attack.

In the toddler two-year-old age grouping, we try to restrict age spread to no more than one year. Thus children range in age from eighteen to thirty months. Children are promoted to the next group, the two-year-olds, when they are able to talk and are ready for toilet training.

The next advancement (to the two-to-three-year-old class) is based on his/her ability to participate in group activities and the rather arbitrary decision that he/she must be toilet trained. The latter requirement is not due to any value judgment placed on toilet training, but rather because toilet facilities are not adjacent to the two-to-three-year-old classroom.

Whatever groupings you establish in your own day care center, you should correlate the grouping with the classroom setup in order to ensure optimal growth and development of your children. Classrooms for infant day care should not duplicate equipment and supplies used by older children. Neither should they attempt to duplicate the home. While elements from both environments are appropriate for this age group, neither contains all elements we feel are most important.

At Castle Square we have tried to develop a curriculum in the following categories. We feel the first five areas are basic components in all preschool programs, while the last five should be included, but may or may not require a specific space or area.

## LARGE MOTOR ACTIVITY AREAS

As an infant matures, he begins to acquire more and more control over his/her physical self. One of the primary tasks of infancy is beginning mastery of motor skills—how to sit, stand, walk, and climb. Therefore, providing opportunities for large-muscle development is extremely important. How do you design an environment which is exciting and stimulating for both your very youngest and very oldest children? How do you prevent conflict when the two groups, infants and toddlers, must coexist in some of the same living space?

As mentioned earlier, we are completely opposed to confining infants to cribs or playpens during waking hours. Instead we suggest you offer the following alternatives:

### Carpeted Platform or "Pit" Area

At Bromley Heath Infant Day Care Center the staff has constructed a large (6 by 9 feet) platform in the corner of one of the playrooms for the use of infants. The platform is bounded on two sides by walls; one has windows, and the children can look at the world outside. The third side has a partial shelf partition, under which children may crawl and look at themselves in a mirror. Colorful mobiles hang above the platform, and pictures adorn the walls. Toys and pillows are scattered around the platform, and infants are free to sit, crawl, play with toys and each other without fear of being run over by older infants speeding about in walkers or on tricycles.

At Castle Square we use a carpeted, sunken pit area for infants. It serves much the same purpose as the raised platform at Bromley Heath; young babies are protected from more mobile, active infants but are still part of the group. When infants are not in the pit area, they are placed in bounce-chairs, bolstered with pillows and towels to a sitting position. From this vantage point they can play with toys on the bounce-chair tray and watch older infants move about. While propped in the bounce-chair, infants can be moved to the area of greatest activity. For example, during summer when older infants and toddlers were splashing about in the wading pool, young infants (two to four months old) sat happily watching them and playing with their rattles and other toys.

### Large Carpeted Area

Half of our floor space for infants at Castle Square is covered with indoor-outdoor carpeting. Here infants crawl around safely and play on the floor with manipulative toys, such as Busy Box and shape-sorters. (See Appendices, page 194, "Manipulative Toys.")

Many infants, before they are able to walk unassisted, enjoy scooting around with walkers. Walkers allow them mobility to investigate their surroundings. For this reason, toys should be stored on low shelves, accessible to children as they crawl, scoot about in walkers, or totter around by themselves.

### Climbing Structures

At Castle Square toddlers climb up and down the three padded stairs we have constructed to reach the laundry-kitchen area. While this kind of climbing seems sufficient at first, toddlers soon want to advance to more complicated climbing apparatus. We have built an indoor climbing structure, allowing infants to climb, slide, and "hide," so they not only exercise but also gain awareness of their bodies in space and the forces acting on them (i.e., gravity, momentum, object permanence).

Our structure contains a little "house" topped by a wide (3 feet) slide approached by an extended ramp. The slide is made of Masonite while the ramp is painted with nonskid deck paint. Toddlers crawl up the ramp and slide down the slide. The wide slide allows them to go down singly or together, and experiment with other ways (head first, sideways, backwards, and so forth). Ordinarily this would be dangerous on a conventional slide, but the Masonite slide slopes gradually, and a thick mat cushions the landing area.

Each of our older toddler and two-year-old classrooms has a modified version of this structure to challenge the older children. In our original two-year-old classroom we installed a metal-runged semicircular climbing device over the indoor sandbox to cushion falls.

In another classroom, we built a platform children reach by climbing a ladderlike ramp. One side is enclosed with heavy fish netting, so children can look out without falling. Another side opens onto a slide ending in the sandbox area.

At present our oldest two-year-old group shares the indoor activity room with the four- and five-year-olds. In this room we have a large structure designed by David Raphael and constructed by David and some of our teachers. A large wide slide adjoins the two-tiered climbing structure. On the back is a truck-tire swing, where two or three children can swing together.

### Tiled Area

Infant-toddlers need exercise throughout the day. They need to run and jump as well as use toys which help develop motor skills. While an outdoor area is most helpful (see chapter 7, "Developing Your Center"), usually children don't have continuous access to it. Moreover, during very bad weather it may not be possible to use the outdoor play area at all. We recommend you have not only a carpeted area for infants but a tile or linoleum area where infant-toddlers can run, jump, ride kiddie cars, tricycles, push cars, or trucks and pull wheeled toys, such as "Snoopy" dogs and "Buzzy" bees.

Toddlers and two-year-olds also need a tiled area to exercise and to ride wheeled vehicles. (See Appendices, page 195, "Suggested Wheeled Toys.")

### Other Areas

Other toys promote large muscle development; for example, infant bounce-chairs, infant "jumpers," rocking boat, assorted soft foam balls, texture balls, Bozo clown punching bag, tumbling mats.

See also the section on outdoor play environment in chapter 7, "Developing Your Center."

For older toddlers, and especially two-year-olds, you may plan some woodworking. Toddlers enjoy toy pounding benches and a carpentry bench (either bought or homemade) where they can pound with a toy hammer, turn "nuts and bolts" with a toy wrench, and so forth.

Two-year-olds may use adult hammers and nails under close supervision. Often children experience sheer joy pounding large-headed nails into soft wood. If wood is unavailable, layers of cardboard glued together will suffice. Sometimes a child will nail two pieces of wood together and call it a train, boat, or car. Praise him/her for such an accomplishment. Children may want to paint their wooden creations and bring them home for the family to admire.

Both our two-year-old and two-to-three-year-old classrooms have a permanent woodworking area. In the two-year-old class-room, children pound on blocks nailed to a shelf. Our two-to-three-year-old classroom has a small carpentry bench equipped with a vise and simple tools such as hammers and saws for use by the children with teacher supervision.

## BLOCK AREA

While infant-toddlers are not as skillful in block construc-tions as older children, they do enjoy piling one block on an-other and, especially, knocking the whole pile down. In our ex-perience, large cardboard building blocks, soft cloth-covered rubber-foam blocks, and giant Lego blocks are all satisfactory for infant-toddlers. We don't recommend traditional wooden nursery blocks with this age group; the structures these children erect are very unsteady and topple over very easily. Moreover, hard blocks hurt when used as weapons or tossed around care-lessly.

Extensive props (rubber people, small cars, trucks) are un-necessary for this age group; infant-toddlers usually find stack-ing and toppling blocks a sufficient challenge.

We do recommend carpeting for the block area, if possible. Moreover, you should try to enclose the area, at least partially, so older infant-toddlers can build without constant interference from younger infants bent on destroying their "towers."

In classrooms with older toddlers and two-year-olds, we use "unit" wooden blocks. Since they are expensive ($100 a set), they should be stored systematically on a nearby shelf. Often "outlining" each shaped block will help children restack blocks in an orderly fashion during cleanup time.

Props for the block area become increasingly important as children get older, for they contribute to rich dramatic play. They include small trucks, cars, and toy animals and people. A list of appropriate blocks and props for various ages can be found in the Appendices, page 196.

## HOUSEKEEPING AREA

Housekeeping is one of the basic areas in all preschool classrooms. Here children find familiar objects most closely related to home, and they act out roles they have seen (mother, father, sister, brother) to gain a better understanding of society. Toddlers especially enjoy role-playing, and both girls and boys love to dress up in simple adult clothing, such as hats, scarves, and pocketbooks and look at themselves in a mirror.

You should have both kitchen and bedroom facilities in your housekeeping area, since these two rooms are the greatest source of identification with home for the child.

Whether you use expensive store-bought furniture or cardboard cartons with appropriate fixtures painted on them, we suggest that your housekeeping "kitchen" contain a sink, stove, refrigerator, table, and a few chairs. And you'll want pots, pans, dishes, broom, and dustpan to encourage dramatic play. These may be purchased from toy manufacturers, donated, or appropriate adult utensils can be substituted.

The "bedroom" should have cradles or beds for assorted dolls; rocking chairs and a storage chest for simple doll clothes (scarves, blankets, poncho-type clothing with only a hole for the doll's head and no snaps, buttons, or sleeves to confuse children). If possible, you should try to make or buy a doll bed large enough for a child to lie in. This encourages dramatic play and the acting out of a most important (if not entirely welcome) aspect of toddler two-year-old life.

We suggest dolls you buy or make be very simple rubber or washable cloth. With these, children are free to use their imagination and make dolls do what they want them to do.

Where you place your housekeeping area depends on many factors—the size and shape of your room, the other areas in the room, and the children's age. The housekeeping area requires little supervision and may bê located near either noisy or quiet areas. One word of caution—if you plan an indoor sand and/or water-play area, do not locate it near housekeeping unless you want both sand and water in with dolls and other equipment.

While our infant-toddler room at Castle Square contains only the most basic housekeeping essentials, our toddler and two-year-old classrooms have large, well-developed housekeeping areas. In the toddler room, the housekeeping area is housed underneath the elevated climbing structure. It's enclosed on three sides and has "windows," creating the illusion of being a little house. In our two-year-old classroom we have a split-level housekeeping area with kitchen on the first floor and bedroom upstairs on a platform behind the kitchen. All structures have been built by our wonderful teaching staff at Castle Square.

To summarize, because language is not highly developed at this age level, toddlers and two-year-olds need to use their entire bodies for learning and expressing themselves. Dramatic play in the housekeeping area is a very important source for role-play. (See Appendices, page 197, for lists of suggested housekeeping furnishings for both high and low budgets.)

## PUZZLE AND TABLE ACTIVITY AREA

Older infants, toddlers, and two-year-olds enjoy group art activities, including finger painting, collage, and play dough. We've found it helpful to have five or six small chairs around a little table for use during art activities, and we usually plan one art session each day.

Young children need to explore the feel, taste, and smell of different objects and materials. Even our middle infants (eight to twelve months) enjoy finger painting with chocolate syrup and whipped cream. Older infant-toddlers can use shaving cream and regular finger paint, with supervision, since they are less likely to put them in their mouths.

Infants, toddlers, and two-year-olds enjoy painting with large half-inch brushes and coloring with large crayons. Sometimes very young infants enjoy it, too. Our son, Evan, at five months "drew" his first picture with a red crayon, "composed" a chocolate finger painting a few days later, and by seven months had made a Christmas tree decoration out of plaster of

Paris and painted it (see picture, page xv). A word of caution: we suggest you store all art supplies out of reach of children. (See Appendices, page 198, for a list of art materials our young children enjoy.)

Before and after art activities the table can be used for puzzles and table games. We're surprised at our infant-toddlers' skill in completing puzzles. Our children progress with surprising speed from very simple one-piece picture puzzles (an apple, a banana) to more difficult multipiece puzzles. We would advise, when choosing puzzles for infant-toddlers, to be sure that each part is a recognizable unit outside the context of the whole puzzle. For example, a piece should be an entire head rather than a piece of head and piece of sky.

Other table games infant-toddlers enjoy are giant attribute blocks (a set of red, yellow, and blue circles, squares, triangles, and rectangles in two sizes and two thicknesses); table blocks (small Lego, colored cubes, parquetry); shape-sorter; stacking toys, and lock box, to mention only a few.

We advise that you display materials on low shelves near the table, so children may select what they want. Don't put all your table toys out at one time. Often children are overwhelmed by too many alternatives and will explore them in only a cursory manner before becoming bored. To keep children interested, introduce new materials often and put old things away for a rest. You can always reintroduce them at a later time. (See Appendices, page 199, for a list of suggested table toys you might find helpful.)

### LIBRARY AREA

Adults can do much to help children develop language skills by talking to them throughout the day—explaining, labeling, and questioning.

In addition, every classroom needs an area specifically for children to look at books and listen to stories. The library area must be cozy and comfortable, a place where children can rest and relax apart from the noise and distraction of other activities. We've found tables and chairs unnecessary here—children feel far more comfortable sprawled on the floor poring over a picture book, or snuggled warmly on an adult's lap while listening to a story. Pillows on the floor, an overstuffed easy chair, and low shelves for book display are all that are needed to provide a relaxed, comfortable reading place.

You shouldn't limit yourself to cloth books, but should include large picture books and others appealing to children's senses. Many have objects to be manipulated, textures to feel, and sometimes pop-out pictures. (See Appendices, pages 200–201, for a list of suggested books for very young children.)

Since books are expensive, you will need to supplement those you purchase with others borrowed from the local library. Children should be taught to care for all books. With proper guidance they will learn to handle all books appropriately.

Two helpful additions to your library area are a felt board and colorful pictures and posters on the wall. All pictures should be hung at child's-eye level and may be actual photographs of your children, simple pictures cut from magazines, or your children's own artwork.

Construct a felt board by simply taping a large piece of felt on the wall or some other flat surface. Smaller shapes from colored felt scraps will adhere to the large felt surface.

The library area should be enclosed, so very young infants cannot crawl in without adult supervision. We've discovered, however, that even very young infants often enjoy sitting on an adult's lap while he/she is reading to other children.

In our toddler classroom the library is housed above the housekeeping area, as part of a two-story structure. Children climb to this retreat away from the hubbub of active play, either to spend a quiet moment or two looking at books or enjoying a one-to-one storytime with a teacher. An elevated library helps young children differentiate between various kinds of space and sense what conduct is appropriate in each area.

## OPTIONAL AREAS

In addition to the five major areas which ought to be a permanent part of every infant-toddler and toddler two-year-old classroom, there are several other options you may want to introduce periodically.

### Sand Play

Infant-toddlers enjoy playing in a small plastic tub or box filled with sterile sand or cornmeal. Children may attempt to eat the sand or cornmeal, but they soon discover the taste and texture are not very pleasant. Very young children can be relied on to experiment, so ordinary beach sand should not be used for this age group.

Both cornmeal and sand used by infant-toddlers should be replaced at least twice a month to prevent mealworms in the cornmeal and an accumulation of dirt and dust in the sandbox.

A word of warning—from our experience, we recommend you use a sand table rather than sandbox for the toddler two-year-old groups. In our first toddler two-year-old classrooms we had a large sandbox area. Children could climb into the sand, cover up their feet, and feel it between their toes. However, we discovered that children in training pants would often visit the sandbox instead of the toilet, just so they would not have to interrupt play. Now we use sand tables that children cannot climb into.

### Water Play

Children enjoy using water both indoors and outside. When used inside, care should be taken to protect children's clothing with plastic smocks. Have newspapers and a mop close by to take care of spills.

Although you may have money to purchase a water-play table, a large plastic wading pool is almost as good and costs a fraction of the price. For further suggestions on water play, see chapter 7, "Developing Your Center," pages 94–95.

### Music

All children respond to music. Even the youngest infant will turn his/her head when hearing a sound. In the infant-toddler classroom, noisemaking materials should be readily available. Infants like rattles, music boxes, and squeeze toys with noisemakers inside, rather than on the outside. Little fingers can detach outside mechanisms, and since everything goes into their mouths, the object may be swallowed or aspirated into the windpipe.

Infant-toddlers love pull toys that clack or chime. And they like drums, bells, tambourines, and shakers. Musical instruments may be purchased or homemade. *The Musical Instrument Recipe Book*, published by The Educational Development Center, Newton, Massachusetts, describes how you can make your own musical instruments for children. (See Appendices, page 205, for a list of musical instruments young children enjoy.)

If possible, it's wonderful to have a record player in every classroom. Naptime is often more pleasant if children can listen to soft music while they go to sleep. Older two-year-olds may enjoy playing records themselves. If teachers permit this activity, children must be taught to take care of both records and machine. This helps keep your own records in good condition, and allows you to borrow records from the local library in good conscience.

A word of warning—never allow the record player to be blaring while no one is listening. It increases the general noise level in the room and serves no useful purpose.

Adults should also sing to and with the children. Toddlers, and especially two-year-olds, love to sing their favorite songs. A teacher doesn't need to have a good singing voice; the fun of singing will make up for any lack of ability. Someone who can play the guitar and sing is a definite asset for your music program, but not essential. If you would like to learn to play a simple instrument we suggest you try the auto-harp. It's a stringed instrument which plays chords when you push numbered buttons with one hand while strumming with the other. Appendix 205 lists records and songs our children find enjoyable.

Not only do children enjoy playing music and singing, they also like to move their bodies to rhythm. With musical instruments, colorful silk scarves, and bright tissue paper, children can express themselves creatively, merging sound, movement, and color.

At Castle Square we were fortunate to have the noted creative movement expert, Norma Canner, author of . . . *And a Time to Dance*, working with our children and staff. She had never "danced" with infants before and wondered if they would respond. All of us were surprised at the natural rhythm and creativity of our infant-toddlers, and Ms. Canner discovered that infants had become one of her favorite groups. Now teachers dance with children, and all experience the sheer joy of creative body movement.

### Science
Science directly and indirectly permeates all aspects of preschool learning. While playing with water, children experiment

and learn about specific gravity (what objects float? what objects sink?). Sand play involves size discrimination (what particles will go through the sifter and how big are the ones left behind?). In music, one hears a variety of tones and tempos. Art activities provide sensory experiences in touch, taste, and smell. In fact, all areas in the classroom give the child opportunities to explore and discover scientific principles.

If science is everywhere, do you need a separate science area? The answer is really up to you, but we believe children of all ages should be exposed to two basics—plants and animals.

For infant-toddlers, we recommend you place plants in sight but out of reach. Often immature infants enjoy ripping off leaves and stuffing them in their mouths. Not only does this ruin the plant but may make a child ill. Obviously, poisonous plants have no place in any preschool classroom or, for that matter, in any home with young children.

Toddlers, and especially two-year-olds, enjoy watching things grow. At Castle Square we have small indoor gardens where children plant grass, beans, carrots, and even tomatoes. Watering plants is a daily ritual most two-year-olds enjoy. Since they are overgenerous with water, try to find plants which tolerate excessive moisture.

Two-year-olds enjoy helping teachers care for animals. They like the daily routine of cleaning cages and feeding the animals. In our two-year-old class we have a rabbit, a guinea pig, and a hamster. It's important to house all animals in sturdy cages, enclosed by screening on all sides for their own protection. Moreover, we advise that you keep animals away from the block and small-manipulative-toy area because sometimes children stuff or drop objects into the animal cages.

Fish tanks should be stored in sight but out of children's reach. One of our two-year-olds hit the glass tank with a hammer, with disastrous results for the fish. Fortunately the child wasn't hurt.

For the benefit of toddler two-year-olds you may want to set up a science display. You and the children can exhibit treasures you have found. Such exhibits might include seashells collected from the beach; leaves, nuts, sticks, and flowers gathered on a walk, or even stones of various sizes and colors. Children enjoy examining these objects, and discussion about them aids the development of language skills.

*Language Development and Mathematical Skills*

Throughout the day children are exposed to language and mathematical skills. While these activities should never be presented formally, they should be part of the classroom program. Scales which balance when an equal number of rings are placed on each side, manipulative toys which call for correct matching of pegs and holes (number-sorter), and finger plays (see Appendices, pages 193–194) all contribute to the development of such concepts, as do many table games and puzzles.

Children enjoy counting out numbers with teachers. If teachers and children recite in unison, the children acquire both language and mathematical skills. Picture Lotto games are fun, especially for two-year-olds, and help build both object recognition and vocabulary. Attractive pictures at child's-eye level throughout the room both elicit questions and develop language skills. Usually language and number materials are not housed in any one classroom area; these skills are taught through informal teacher-child interaction and play.

## SUMMARY

In this chapter we have sought to describe those classroom areas we feel are most important in promoting optimal child growth and development. We have described how the physical environment can help children exercise their muscles and develop physical coordination as well as promote cognitive development. However, the true test of the effectiveness of any environment influencing young children lies in the quality of the adult-child relationship. If you have a quality staff, interested and knowledgeable about young children, you have the basic ingredient for a good program. If you add an environment designed specifically with young children in mind—with areas where they are free to explore and learn—you have the other essential ingredient for promoting optimal child growth and development.

You may have wondered why we haven't mentioned television for infant-toddler day care programs. We feel TV has no place in quality daily care of infants for the following reasons:

1. If you employ a quality teaching staff, active adult-child involvement is much more important for child development than TV programs.

2. Both infants and toddlers are egocentric, interested in themselves and in interacting with other children and with toys, rather than watching television passively.

3. We believe television develops a passive spirit, stifling creativity and individuality.

4. Since infant-toddlers have short attention spans, very few programs hold their interest.

5. Spectator orientation runs counter to the goals of a quality infant program allowing infants freedom to explore, experiment, and learn.

6. We fear TV will be used as a crutch by inexperienced teachers, thus encouraging custodial baby-sitting care.

7. Finally, since most children will be exposed to television at home, we feel day care should offer children something more challenging than just a rehash of experiences already provided in the home.

Naturally your classroom will depend on the actual design of your center, the personnel you employ, the needs of your children, and the amount of money you can afford to spend to develop classrooms suitable for very young children.

CHAPTER TEN

# Associated Services

## INTRODUCTION

In order to furnish comprehensive child care and provide
for the child's physical, mental, social, and emotional needs,
you will have to supplement your day-care program with various associated services. Depending upon the needs of your children and their families, you may establish such services at the
center, assist parents to locate such services in the community,
or adopt a compromise between these two extremes. Whatever
your decision, you must be responsible for the total well-being
of each of your children.

Some states have legislated minimum requirements for ensuring that children in day care receive such supportive services. We hope that you will not be content with these basic suggestions, but will seek to develop a comprehensive program
based on the needs of your "special" children.

This chapter will discuss the components which supplement
a quality child care program. To simplify the problem, we
have broken down the associated services into the following
areas: medical care, nutrition, dental care, social, and psychological services. We repeat—a quality care program for infants
must assure that these services are provided.

Since our experience has been chiefly with children at the
Castle Square Center, we have used this center to illustrate the
kinds of associated services we believe are necessary. Our program should not necessarily be used as a model. Add to or sub-
tract from these services in accordance with the needs of your
own community.

## HEALTH AND MEDICAL CARE SERVICES

Although the goal of a quality day care center should be to make sure that each child is receiving comprehensive medical care, some centers may decide that their role is to encourage family-oriented health care, and may assist the child's family to arrange care for the entire family. Where a family does not have access to health care, the social worker or director must assist parents to arrange for this care either from a private physician or a nearby clinic.

At Castle Square, we require routine physical examinations and up-to-date immunizations of all children. Infants and toddlers must be seen every three months; children aged two to three years, every six months; and children over age three, annually. The parent may desire the child's own pediatrician or clinic to perform examinations and immunizations, or may give permission for our pediatrician to provide these services. Before any child is admitted he must be examined by a physician, who fills out our Medical Report Form. (See Appendices, pages 179–182.)

Our pediatrician, Dr. Norman Bell, visits the center every other week. At this time he performs routine physical examinations (with parental permission), examines any child whom teachers may refer for health evaluation, and prescribes medications as needed. He refers children to their family doctor or health clinic for treatment if necessary. The pediatrician also supervises infant feeding schedules and speaks with parents individually during routine examinations and at parent group meetings. Moreover, he conducts an in-service training program in first aid and instructs teachers how to recognize common childhood diseases.

No matter how you arrange for health care, we feel the following aspects should be covered to insure comprehensive services:

1. Parents must provide the center with the name, address, and telephone number of the person to be contacted in an emergency when parents cannot be reached. (See application form, page 188.)
2. The center must keep on file a complete preadmission

examination on each child. This record should contain a complete health history, complete physical examination, record of immunizations given, formula or special dietary requirements when necessary, and an evaluative statement.

3. The center must be sure that immunizations are up to date. This means the child must not only have received the original course of injections, but also boosters at appropriate intervals. Most states require immunization for the following:

   a. Diphtheria, pertussis (whooping cough), and tetanus —DPT: first shot at two to three months; second and third at one-month intervals. Boosters are given at eighteen months and five years
   b. Smallpox, if recommended, at six to twelve months
   c. Oral Trivalent Polio: first dose at age two to three months; second at four to five months; third, as recommended, at ten to twelve months
   d. Measles at age twelve months

4. The center must secure medical attention for a sick child, and advise parents to keep the child at home until he is entirely free from disease. This policy protects the sick child as well as the other children in the day care center. (See Appendices, pages 185–186, "Sample Letters to Parents.") Since the following symptoms are signs of possible impending infection or disease which may be contagious to other children, parents should be advised to seek prompt medical attention for their child if he has any of these symptoms and keep him home while he is ill, to avoid exposing others.

   a. Signs of a new cold: fever, cough, running nose, watery eyes, sore throat
   b. Diarrhea
   c. Inflammation of the eyes (conjunctivitis)
   d. Abscess
   e. Draining sores or burns
   f. Rash (until cause is diagnosed and determined non-contagious)
   g. Headache or head pain
   h. Vomiting

    i.  Loss of appetite

    j.  Excessive irritability or unusual passivity

5. Some states require a doctor's permission for readmission to day care after a child has recovered from certain communicable diseases. Check your rules and regulations regarding readmission requirements. In any case, parents should be notified if a contagious disease occurs at the center. At Castle Square we have form letters, which we give to parents, describing the most common contagious childhood diseases. (See Appendices, pages 185–186, "Sample Letters to Parents.")

6. The center must provide an isolation room for the child who presents symptoms of illness during the day. The child should remain excluded from the group until he can be taken home by his parents, or until other arrangements can be made for his care.

7. The center must arrange for emergency care of children as per agreement with parents. All centers should have a written plan for handling emergencies and injuries, and slips for emergency care of each child signed by his parents. (See Appendices, page 183, "Permission Slip: Emergency Medical Care.") In addition, the emergency-care procedure for all children should be outlined and posted in each classroom. (See Appendices, page 184, "Emergency Care Procedure.")

8. The center should either have a nurse on its staff or train teachers to provide simple first-aid treatment of injuries. All injuries must be recorded and parents informed of the injury that same day. (See Appendices, page 184, "Accident Report Form.")

9. The center should have a locked first-aid cabinet which contains basic first-aid supplies and equipment. We suggest that you include the following:

    a.  Ointments: Vaseline, Desitin

    b.  Surgical supplies: bandage scissors, sterilizing basin with cover, pickup forceps

    c.  Dressings: sterile cotton, Ace bandages, gauze squares, assorted widths of roller gauze, cotton-tipped applicators, assorted widths of adhesive tape, assorted sized Band-Aids, tongue depressors

    d. Solutions: calamine lotion (USP), pHiSoHex, alcohol 70 percent, hydrogen peroxide, aqueous Zephiran

    e. Miscellaneous: scale, ice bag, thermometers (both rectal and oral)

10. The center staff should give medications to a child when necessary, but only on written order from a physician. Such medications must be labeled with the child's name, name of the drug, and directions for its administration. All medications should be stored in the locked first-aid cabinet and discarded or returned to parents when no longer needed.

11. The center should provide screening programs for vision, hearing, lead poisoning, speech, and tuberculosis.

12. The center should ensure that all staff personnel are in good health.

    a. Before beginning employment, and every year thereafter, each staff member should receive a physical examination and secure a health certificate signed by his/her physician. This certificate should state that the individual has been examined and that there is no apparent illness present which might adversely affect the children in his/her care at the center. These certificates should be kept up to date and on file at the center.

    b. Before beginning work all staff personnel should submit an authorized report of a negative intradermal tuberculin test. Chest X-rays are contraindicated because of radiation buildup from periodic testing. Tests should be repeated every three years unless shorter intervals are medically indicated to determine freedom from tuberculosis in a communicable form.

    c. No staff member should work with children if he or she has an upper-respiratory infection, gastrointestinal illness, or other contagious disease.

13. The center must ensure that all staff members follow sanitary procedures while caring for young children.

    a. Available handwashing facilities should be well supplied with soap and disposable hand towels.

Hands must be washed after and between such activities as changing a child and feeding him.

b. There should be individual towels and washcloths for each child. Infants require two washcloths, one for face and one for bottom unless disposable cloths are used and discarded after each use. All cloths and towels should be washed and dried daily.

c. Bed linens should be kept clean, changed regularly and also whenever they are soiled. Each child should use only his own bedding.

d. Toys and equipment used by infants should be washed routinely.

e. All items used by sick children must be cleaned and disinfected before reuse.

## NUTRITIONAL SERVICES

Recent studies indicate that the one factor which can most influence a child's development during his first three years of life is nutrition. Not only is it essential that the child receive proper nutrition for his brain development, but also his mother's nutrition during pregnancy is of vital significance.

We know now that the human brain develops in four successive stages. In early intrauterine growth, the brain grows bigger, and the cells divide and redivide. After birth occurs, brain cells divide less rapidly, but the existing cells grow larger in size. By the end of the first year of life, brain cells stop dividing, and all growth comes from an increase in cell size, not number. Finally, the fourth stage occurs between the ages of eighteen and twenty-four months, when connections are formed between the cells. It is believed that the number of connections between cells are even more important than the actual number of brain cells.

Malnutrition at any point during gestation and the first two years of life retards brain cell development permanently. Therefore, adequate nutrition is a critical factor if infants are to develop to their potential. After these early years in infancy, the brain never gets another chance to grow. For this reason, the degree to which a child is able to reach his inborn potential will depend to a large extent upon how adequate his nutrition has been during the first forty-five months of his life.

Centers which care for young children during the day must assume the responsibility for ensuring that they receive nourishing meals. However, the nutritional responsibilities of the center do not conclude with the provision of an adequate diet. Care must be taken that food is prepared simply and served attractively, so that children will enjoy eating.

We know that food carries an emotional impact to children. Familiar foods link memories of home to mealtime at the center, and promote security and feelings of belonging. Eating can also be a learning experience for children; they need time to experience new tastes and textures and learn to enjoy a variety of foods. Mealtime, therefore, should be unhurried and pleasant—a time for enjoying the food and talking with other children.

### Food Requirements

Children enrolled in day care usually receive a substantial part of their daily food requirements at the center. Depending upon the length of time a child spends in the center, snacks and sometimes meals need to be provided. The variety and amount of food to be served should meet the National Research Council Food Allowances for children in day care.

For a child in a half-day care center (under four hours) a midmorning or midafternoon snack of milk or juice and bread, or its equivalent, is sufficient. Children in day care five to eight hours require that one-third to one-half of their food needs for the day be served in one regular meal (not counting breakfast) and one or more snacks. For children in day care longer than nine hours, two-thirds of their food requirements for the day need to be provided through two meals and one or more snacks.

The minimal amounts of food to be served at meals depend upon the age of the child. Formula and diet schedules for infants should be prescribed by a doctor and conscientiously followed at home and in the center. Individual diet cards for young infants need to be kept on file and revised frequently by the doctor as the infant matures.

The Special Food Service Program for Children in each state receives donated (surplus or commodity) foods from the federal Department of Agriculture, and makes arrangements for such foods to be distributed to needy families and service institutions for children, such as nonprofit child-care centers. The following minimum amounts of component foods to be served at meals are suggested.

### Age one to three years

Breakfast: ½ cup of milk; ¼ cup of juice or fruit; ½ slice of bread or equivalent; ¼ cup of cereal or an equivalent quantity of both bread and cereal.

Lunch or Supper: ½ cup of milk; 1 ounce (edible portion as served) of meat or an equivalent quantity of an alternate; ¼ cup of vegetable or fruits or both consisting of two or more kinds; ½ slice of bread or equivalent; ½ teaspoon of butter or fortified margarine.

Supplemental Food: ½ cup of milk or juice; ½ slice of bread or equivalent.

At Castle Square, our nutritionist, Mary-Brenda Cortell', has prepared an infant feeding program which we follow unless we receive specific orders to the contrary from the child's physician. Because parents and staff alike have found this booklet helpful, we pass it on to you in the hope that you may find it useful. (See Appendices, pages 174–178, "Infant Feeding Program.")

### Reimbursement

Section 13 of the National School Lunch Act, as amended in 1968, provides funds for reimbursement to service institutions for meals served to children. Such "service institutions" include child-care centers which provide day-care services to children from poor economic areas, or neighborhoods where there are large numbers of working mothers.

Reimbursement rates are determined by the State Office of School Lunch when proper application is made. Maximum rates of reimbursement per child for meals are as follows: breakfast, fifteen cents; lunch or supper, thirty cents; and supplemental foods, ten cents.

Funds are available also to pay 75 percent of the purchase or rental of equipment for storage, preparation, transportation, and serving of food to children. For further information on reimbursement possibilities, consult the State Office of School Lunch Programs in your vicinity.

### Refrigeration and Storage

There must be some provision for the refrigeration and storage of food supplies at the center. Milk and all perishable foods should be stored in a refrigerator maintained at 45° Fahrenheit or below. Food supplies not refrigerated must be kept in clean, covered containers which- are inaccessible to insects and rodents.

### Sanitary Procedures

Persons preparing and serving meals should submit to the center a health certificate signed by a physician stating that they are in good health and free from any communicable disease which might be passed on to others via food products. They should maintain good sanitary practices at all times; wash hands thoroughly with soap and warm water before preparing food; wear a clean, washable uniform, apron or dress daily; handle food with clean utensils in a sanitary manner.

All eating and drinking utensils should be free from cracks or chips and be maintained and stored in a sanitary condition. Utensils used in preparation, serving, and eating should be washed with soap or detergent in warm water and then sanitized. Equipment should be air dried, since bacteria can accumulate on dish towels and be spread from one utensil to another.

### Summary

A quality child-care center insures that children's nutritional needs are met and that mealtime is a happy occasion for sampling new foods and developing new skills. Therefore, it will be the responsibility of the center to do the following:

1. Provide all formulas, meals, and supplemental snacks as necessary to the children enrolled in the day care center

2. Assist parents in learning how to provide the proper foods for their children through arranging for a nutritionist to speak at a parents' meeting, conducting demonstrations using surplus foods, menu-planning with parents either individually or as a group

3. Plan meals and supplements so they are well balanced

and in accordance with the National Research Council Food Allowances for children in day care

4. Utilize the services of a nutritionist for menu-planning and supervision of kitchen staff

5. Post menus weekly so mothers can plan for meals at home accordingly

6. Provide a kitchen where food can be properly prepared and stored. The kitchen should be separate from the classrooms and used only for the preparation and storage of food, and the washing, sanitizing, and storage of eating utensils and equipment. The kitchen should be kept clean and orderly, and have adequate lighting and ventilation. In addition, sinks with hot and cold running water, refrigeration, cooking range, and shelves for storage should be provided

7. Utilize surplus and wholesale foods in order to reduce food costs

8. Receive reimbursement, if possible, for food and equipment costs under the terms of the National School Lunch Act

9. Provide a pleasant relaxed atmosphere at mealtimes, so that children may enjoy eating and sharing conversations

10. Provide vitamin supplements (with written parental permission)

11. Ensure that all staff members working with food submit a report from a physician stating that they are in good health and are free from any communicable disease which might be passed on to others via food products, and a report of a negative intradermal tuberculin test

12. Ensure that all staff members follow prescribed sanitary procedures regarding the preparation and storage of food, and the sanitizing of equipment and utensils

## DENTAL CARE SERVICES

Dental care for children should begin in the early preschool years. By the time a child is two years old, he should have routine dental examinations and cleanings. A preschool child can become familiar with the dentist and learn not to fear him. In addition, cavities or other problems which may be found in the first teeth can be corrected before they affect the child's permanent teeth.

It will be up to you to determine whether the role of your center is to maintain an environment which fosters good dental health, or whether it will provide comprehensive dental care to all children enrolled at the center through direct dental services. Your decision will be based on the needs of the children at your center, the wishes of their parents, the availability of good dental care, and how much the center's budget can afford.

At Castle Square we have made arrangements with the Boston Dispensary, Tufts New England Medical Center, so that children enrolled in our center receive dental care. In this connection, we have instituted the following plan for providing preventive dental services:

1. A dentist (postgraduate student) from the Boston Dispensary speaks at a parents' meeting to discuss preventive dental care.
2. This dentist, or another from the Boston Dispensary, conducts several in-service training sessions in preventive care for the teaching staff.
3. For those parents interested in the preventive dental program, the Boston Dispensary provides the following services to children enrolled at the day care center:
   a. Screening children aged two to five. Dentist comes to the day care center to examine children to see if they have any dental problems.
   b. Appointments are scheduled at the Boston Dispensary for prophylactic fluoride and X-rays. Parents accompany children and teachers, at least for the first visit.
   c. Children requiring dental treatment receive care at the Dispensary.

## SOCIAL SERVICES

The need for some social service is vital to any program serving young children and their families. Whether your center employs a social worker on a full-time, part-time, or consultant basis, this important service should not be neglected.

If you have a small program, the director usually assumes the responsibilities entailed in a social service component. In large centers, like Castle Square, there is need for an experienced, mature social worker. She is responsible for fulfilling the following functions:

1. Reviewing all applications and interviewing prospective children and their parents

2. Obtaining information regarding:
   a. Reasons for seeking day-care services
   b. Family background information
   c. Pertinent developmental history (see application form in Appendices, pages 187–192)

3. Explaining the services offered by the center:
   a. Hours of operation
   b. Fees
   c. Policies
   d. Admission process
   e. Responsibilities of parents and responsibilities assumed by the center for health and medical care, nutritional services, dental care, social services, and psychological services
   f. Child-care program

4. Referring to community agencies problems noted at home or at school that cannot be resolved by the center

5. Keeping parents informed of their child's adjustment and experiences in the day-care program, and working closely with parents to ensure optimal integration of home experiences with the day-care program

6. Observing children, and helping teachers and parents understand the meaning of individual behavior

7. Providing the opportunity for parent participation in the day care center: assisting in the classrooms, helping to determine policies at the center, setting up agenda for meetings, and so forth

## PSYCHOLOGICAL SERVICES

Mental hygiene encompasses the whole child; his physical, emotional, and social well-being and that of his family. The classroom program itself can do much to nurture the psychological development of children through a child-centered program sensitive to their needs and abilities. Thus one can view "psychological services" as an integral program component.

There are three main aspects of mental hygiene which can be promoted within the classroom. The first is the establishment of an intangible quality called "atmosphere." Love is perhaps its most vital ingredient; but loving care alone is not enough to produce positive psychological growth. The reassurance of firm but kind adult guidance is needed, as is a discipline which builds inner strength and social awareness in the child.

Under no circumstances should adults resort to chastisement, corporal punishment, or ridicule of a child. These forms of discipline are exceedingly detrimental because they undermine the child's sense of worth by causing humiliation and frustration. Redirecting the child's attention and removing him from the group until he has regained control are two methods of discipline which promote healthy psychological growth.

Good teacher-parent relationships are the third ingredient necessary to enhance the psychological development of the child in day care. As the child is the focus of both the staff and the parents, the two should cooperate to promote healthy family relationships. Sometimes harmful attitudes can be changed through patient parent counseling.

Whether or not you provide the services of a psychologist, your center must provide a healthy environment for emotional and mental growth. We feel each center should provide the first two functions listed, and the others if possible.

1. Creating a warm, loving, child-centered atmosphere which is responsive to the needs of individual children

2. Working closely with parents in order to understand the child and his needs more completely

3. Providing the services of a psychologist to—
   a. Observe the classroom groups periodically and follow up individual children;
   b. Study the progress records kept by the nurse, doctor, dentist, and teachers on each child enrolled in the center;
   c. Periodically test children in order to record developmental gains and evaluate the components of the care program;
   d. Organize staff conferences to coordinate the associated services and evaluate their effects on individual children;
   e. Speak to parents in groups in order to discuss some of the characteristics of child growth and development, and to try to answer any questions parents may have;
   f. Arrange conferences with parents to discuss their child and his progress;
   g. Refer children and/or their parents for psychiatric evaluation and treatment whenever necessary

4. To provide the services of a psychiatrist to—
   a. Consult with the staff regarding the mental health aspects of child care, and offer specific advice concerning children with behavior or personality problems;
   b. Make referrals for evaluation and treatment of the child and/or his parents if such care cannot be provided at the center

# Parent Cooperative Infant Care Centers

Throughout this book we have been describing good infant care mainly by citing examples derived from infant units which are part of larger day care centers. We have followed this policy for two reasons. First, we believe that infant-toddlers profit from the experience of having older children around, particularly if the children involved are siblings; and secondly, our experience has been mainly in developing and operating a large day care center.

On the other hand, we realize that for at least several years, while the rules and regulations are being revised, infant day care will operate mainly in homes and one-classroom centers. Moreover, there will be some parents who will prefer to have their infants in small centers close to home. We think alternate choices ought to be available; therefore, in order to help parents who wish to organize an infant center for their children, we shall attempt to show how the information presented in the preceding chapters may be utilized efficiently. Again, we repeat, only you, the organizers, can adapt the suggestions offered in this book to your own particular needs.

All programs enrolling infants must conform to the particular standards of each state (see Appendices, pages 144–145, for licensing agencies by state). This means that whether or not your small parent cooperative is located in a house, apartment, or church classroom, it must meet all the rules and regulations for group infant care in your state.

Once you are familiar with the requirements for infant day care in your state, you can begin your search for money to develop and operate your center. It should be readily apparent that you will not need a very substantial amount of initial capital (just a month's rent, if you cannot find free space; some toys and equipment, if they have not been donated already, and one month's salary for the teacher, if you employ one). Fund-raising drives (see chapter 5, "Preparing a Budget and Raising Funds") should be sufficient to raise enough money to get your center in operation. Operating costs can be met through a combination of tuition fees and periodic fund-raising activities.

Once you have secured some "seed money," you are ready to begin looking for a location to house your center. Because you will need only one classroom, you may be able to convince a local church or business to donate the necessary space. Even if you find that you must rent space, your outlay for this budget item should be substantially lower than it is for the larger centers. (For further suggestions see chapter 6, "Locating Your Center.")

The largest budget item in most programs, staffing your center, should not be of particular concern to you, as parents will provide free teaching assistance. Even if you do have one professional teacher (we strongly recommend this policy), this expense should be the only personnel cost you will have to meet. Since parents will provide for all the health, social, and psychological needs of their own children, your center need not worry about an associated services staff.

If you do not plan to hire a professional teacher, you will need to select one parent as head teacher. He/she will be responsible for establishing the daily plan of program operations and coordinating all parent-teacher time schedules.

We recommend that parents submit in writing the periods of time when they are available to devote a large block of time for teaching (no less than four hours). Once the schedule of parent teaching has been arranged you should try to adhere to it, as young children are upset by the constant coming and going of ever changing adult caretakers. Children need to feel that their world is a reliable, predictable place that they can count on. With a fixed schedule for parent teachers, children can prepare themselves for changes which occur on a regular basis.

If you employ a professional teacher, he/she will be responsible for providing in-service education to parent teachers. In addition to the professional teacher, and especially if your center is staffed by parents only, we recommend that you have professionals (doctors, psychologists, and so forth) consult with your staff regularly. Since you may not be able to convince consultants to offer their services free, you may wish to set aside some money to hire them. If your financial situation is shaky, you might form parent study groups and devise your own in-service teacher training and staff development program based on suggestions in chapter 8, "Teacher Training," in the earlier book, *Day Care*.*

Moreover, we cannot emphasize too strongly that you should select parents for teaching positions who are qualified by personality and temperament to work with young children. See chapter 8, "Staffing Your Program," for desirable characteristics of teachers.

Not all parents will be able or wish to offer teaching time to your program. You should encourage them to contribute to the program in some other way. Other responsibilities which need to be covered in operating a day care center for infants include raising funds for program operation; securing materials, supplies, and equipment by donation; constructing classroom areas; repairing toys and equipment; general handyman duties and maintenance; office work (typing records and correspondence, paying bills, bookkeeping); preparing meals; providing transportation.

While the majority of your toys and equipment may be donated, you still may want to supplement your program with purchased or homemade materials. See chapter 9, "Developing the Classrooms for Infant-Toddlers and Toddler Two-Year-Olds," and the lists of suggested equipment, materials, and supplies in the attached appendix.

Your food-service costs will be minimal if you require parents to furnish their child's food. In this case, you will need only a small refrigerator for storing home-furnished food, and perhaps a hot plate for heating such simple foods as soup. However, we suggest that if your program is this tiny, you might have one of the parents prepare meals at the center. If your group is located in an apartment, house, or church, this should present no problem. Otherwise, you will need a small utility kitchen to prepare simple hot meals.

* E. Belle Evans, Beth Shub, and Marlene Weinstein, *Day Care* (Boston: Beacon Press, 1971), pp. 67–89.

Travel expenses will be borne by parents, who should be responsible for bringing their children to the center and picking them up. Informal arrangements such as car pools can be handled by the parents themselves, or two parents may offer to provide transportation as part of their contribution to the center. We say *two* parents because we feel that very young children need one adult to supervise while the other drives.

An example of how your budget might look for a small parent cooperative center with sixteen infant-toddlers is as follows:

|  | High Budget | Low Budget |
|---|---|---|
| *Staff* | | |
| Head teacher (full-time) | $8,000 | $8,000 |
| Parent teachers (quarter-time each) | | |
| Fringe benefits @ 10% | 800 | 800 |
| Administrative costs @ 5% | 400 | Donated |
| *Staff subtotal* | $9,200 | $8,800 |
| | | |
| *Consultants* @ $50 x 12 months | $ 600 | |
| | | |
| *Equipment* | | |
| Educational | 500 | |
| Caretaking and housekeeping | 400 | |
| Office | 100 | |
| Kitchen | 200 | |
| Woodworking | 200 | |
| *Equipment subtotal* | $1,400 | Donated |
| | | |
| *Supplies* | | |
| Educational | 100 | |
| Caretaking and housekeeping | 800 | |
| Office | 100 | |
| *Supplies subtotal* | $1,000 | Donated |
| | | |
| *Food* | | |
| 60¢ x 16 children x 260 days | $2,496 | Donated |

|                                                                                                        | High Budget | Low Budget |
|--------------------------------------------------------------------------------------------------------|-------------|------------|
| *Space*                                                                                                |             |            |
| 710 sq. ft. (35 sq. ft./child = 560 sq. ft. plus 150 sq. ft. for kitchen and toilets) @ $2.50 per sq. ft. | $1,775      | Donated    |
|                                                                                                        |             |            |
| *Utilities*                                                                                            |             |            |
| Telephone @ $15 per month                                                                              | 180         | 180        |
| Heat @ $12 per month                                                                                   | 144         | 144        |
| Light @ $10 per month                                                                                  | 120         | 120        |
| *Utilities subtotal*                                                                                   | $   444     | $   444    |
|                                                                                                        |             |            |
| *Total*                                                                                                | $16,915     | $9,244     |

From the foregoing example it is apparent that a low-budget parent cooperative infant center can be operated with parents paying less than $15 per child per week, while a high-budget program will cost at least $20. Your actual operating costs will depend upon your specific expenses and upon the amount of donated time, space, equipment, supplies, and materials. So long as you maintain optimal care for your children as the primary program goal, the need for a quality staff, appropriate materials and equipment, and the development of an exciting learning environment for your infants remain the same no matter what the size and scope of your center.

## APPENDICES

### DAY CARE LICENSING BY STATE

| State | State Licensing Agency |
|---|---|
| Alabama | Dept. of Welfare: Pensions and Security |
| Alaska | Depts. of Health and Welfare |
| Arizona | Dept. of Health |
| Arkansas | Dept. of Public Welfare |
| California | Dept. of Welfare: Social Welfare |
| Colorado | Dept. of Welfare: Social Services |
| Connecticut | Dept. of Health |
| Delaware | Dept. of Health and Social Services |
| District of Columbia | Dept. of Public Health |
| Florida | Health and Rehabilitative Services |
| Georgia | Dept. of Welfare: Family and Children Services |
| Hawaii | Dept. of Welfare: Social Services and Housing |
| Idaho | Dept. of Welfare: Public Assistance |
| Illinois | Dept. of Welfare: Children and Family Services |
| Indiana | Dept. of Public Welfare |
| Iowa | Dept. of Welfare: Social Services |
| Kansas | Dept. of Health |
| Kentucky | Dept. of Welfare: Child Welfare |
| Louisiana | Dept. of Public Welfare |
| Maine | Depts. of Health and Welfare |
| Maryland | Depts. of Health and Mental Hygiene |
| Massachusetts | Dept. of Public Health: Division of Family Health Services |
| Michigan | Dept. of Welfare: Social Services |
| Minnesota | Dept. of Public Welfare |
| Mississippi | Dept. of Public Welfare |
| Missouri | Depts. of Public Health and Welfare |

| *State* | *State Licensing Agency* |
|---|---|
| Montana | Dept. of Public Welfare |
| Nebraska | Dept. of Welfare |
| Nevada | Depts. of Health, Welfare and Rehabilitation |
| New Hampshire | Depts. of Health and Welfare |
| New Jersey | Dept. of Education |
| New Mexico | Dept. of Health and Social Services |
| New York | Dept. of Welfare: Social Services |
| No. Carolina | Dept. of Social Services |
| No. Dakota | Dept. of Public Welfare |
| Ohio | Dept. of Welfare |
| Oklahoma | Dept. of Welfare |
| Oregon | Dept. of Welfare |
| Pennsylvania | Dept. of Welfare |
| Rhode Island | Dept. of Welfare: Social and Rehabilitative Services |
| So. Carolina | Dept. of Public Welfare |
| So. Dakota | Dept. of Welfare |
| Tennessee | Dept. of Welfare |
| Texas | Dept. of Welfare |
| Utah | Dept. of Welfare |
| Vermont | Economic Opportunity |
| Virginia | Dept. of Welfare and Institutions |
| Washington | Dept. of Welfare: Public Assistance |
| W. Virginia | Dept. of Welfare |
| Wisconsin | Dept. of Health and Social Services |
| Wyoming | Dept. of Public Welfare |

## MAXIMUM NUMBER OF INFANTS PER ADULT BY AGE OF CHILDREN

| State | Number of Infants per Teaching Staff | | | | |
|---|---|---|---|---|---|
| | Under 1 | 1-1½ | 1½-2 | 2-2½ | 2½-3 |
| Alabama | 5 | 5 | 5 | 5 | 5 |
| Alaska | 5 | 5 | 5 | 5 | 5 |
| Arizona | 10 | 10 | 10 | 10 | 10 |
| Arkansas | 4 | 4 | 4 | 6 | 6 |
| California | – | – | – | 12 | 12 |
| Colorado | – | – | – | – | 8 |
| Connecticut | 4 | 4 | 4 | 4 | 4 |
| Delaware | 5 | 8 | 8 | 8 | 15 |
| District of Columbia | 6 | 6 | 10 | 10 | 10 |
| Florida | 5 | 5 | 5 | 10 | 10 |
| Georgia | 7 | 7 | 10 | 10 | 10 |
| Hawaii | – | – | – | 10 | 10 |
| Idaho | – | – | – | – | 10 |
| Illinois | 6 | 6 | 6 | 8 | 8 |
| Indiana | – | – | – | – | – |
| Iowa | – | – | – | 6 | 6 |
| Kansas | – | – | – | – | – |
| Kentucky | 6 | 6 | 6 | 8 | 8 |
| Louisiana | 6 | 6 | 14 | 14 | 14 |
| Maine | – | – | – | – | 8 |
| Maryland | Not specified under licensing requirements | | | | |
| Massachusetts | – | – | – | – | – |
| Michigan | – | – | – | – | 10 |
| Minnesota | 10 | 10 | 10 | 10 | 10 |
| Mississippi | – | – | – | 8 | 8 |
| Missouri | – | – | – | – | – |
| Montana | – | – | – | 15 | 15 |
| Nebraska | – | – | – | – | – |
| Nevada | 2 | 2 | 2 | 10 | 10 |
| New Hampshire | – | – | – | – | – |
| New Jersey | – | – | – | Not specified | |
| New Mexico | 10 | 10 | 10 | 15 | 15 |

| State | Number of Infants per Teaching Staff | | | | |
|---|---|---|---|---|---|
| | *Under 1* | *1-1½* | *1½-2* | *2-2½* | *2½-3* |
| New York | 4 | 4 | 5 | 5 | 5 |
| No. Carolina | 5 | 8 | 8 | 12 | 12 |
| No. Dakota | 3 | 3 | 3 | 5 | 5 |
| Ohio | 8 | 8 | 10 | 10 | 10 |
| Oklahoma | 4 | 6 | 6 | 8 | 8 |
| Oregon | 10 | 10 | 10 | 10 | 10 |
| Pennsylvania | – | – | – | – | – |
| Rhode Island | – | – | – | – | – |
| So. Carolina | 6 | 6 | 6 | 8 | 8 |
| So. Dakota | 8 | 8 | 8 | 8 | 8 |
| Tennessee | – | – | – | 10 | 10 |
| Texas | 4 | 4 | 4 | 8 | 8 |
| Utah | – | – | – | 10 | 10 |
| Vermont | 2 | 2 | 2 | 6-8 | 6-8 |
| Virginia | 3 | 3 | 3 | 10 | 10 |
| Washington | – | – | – | – | 10 |
| West Virginia | – | – | – | 8 | 8 |
| Wisconsin | 3 | 4 | 4 | 6 | 8 |
| Wyoming | – | – | – | – | – |

## SUGGESTED GENERAL CURRICULUM FURNISHINGS AND EQUIPMENT

|  | High Budget | Low Budget |
|---|---|---|
| *Sleeping Area* | | |
| *Cribs with mattresses (Childcraft) | $ 50.00 ea. | Built in wall |
| Aluminum cots with poly-propylene covers (Childcraft) | 16.00 ea. | $16.00 |
| *Clothes hamper | 15.00 ea. | 15.00 |
| *Rocking chairs | 35.00 ea. | 35.00 |
| Change Table | 25.00 | Homemade |
| | | |
| *Eating Area* | | |
| Plastic-top table (Childcraft) | 34.00 | Homemade |
| *Armchairs (Community) | 13.00 ea. | 13.00 |
| *Feeding tables | 36.00 ea. | 36.00 |
| Small child-size chairs (Childcraft) | 12.00 ea. | Homemade |
| | | |
| *Large-Muscle Activity Area* | | |
| Rocking boat | 35.00 | 35.00 |
| Cellar door playhouse (Child Life) | 179.00 | Homemade |
| *Bounce-chairs | 15.00 ea. | 15.00 |
| Tumbling mats | 30.00 | |
| Pair of stairs (Community) | 36.50 | 30.00 |
| Sand and water-play table | 70.00 | 5.00 Plastic tub |
| Bozo punching bag (Childcraft) | 3.50 | 3.50 |
| *Cosco playpens | 26.00 ea. | 26.00 |
| *Hoola-Coupe walker | 16.00 ea. | 16.00 |
| Vari-play triangle set | 50.00 | Omit |

*For infants only.

|  | High Budget | Low Budget |
|---|---|---|
| *Table Game Area* | | |
| Small table (Childcraft) | 34.00 | Homemade (plywood top) |
| Small chairs (Childcraft) | 12.00 | Homemade (stools) |
| Multistorage unit (Community) | 105.00 | Homemade (crates) |
| Storage shelves (Community) | 54.50 | Homemade (crates) |
| | | |
| *Library* | | |
| Nylon carpet | 10.00 | Donated |
| Large floor pillow | 12.00 | Homemade |
| Mini-library display unit (Childcraft) | 24.00 | Homemade |
| Large comfortable arm-chair | Donated | Donated |
| | | |
| *Miscellaneous* | | |
| Individual storage cubbies (Community) (set of 4 lockers) | 70.00 ea. | Homemade |
| †Carpentry workbench and vise (Community) | 46.50 | Homemade |
| †Set of tools | 62.50 | Donated |

---

†For two-year-olds only.

## SUGGESTED CLASSROOM SUPPLIES AND MATERIALS

*Caretaking*
      \*Quilted crib mattress pads               $1.57 ea.
      \*Fitted crib sheets                  3.50 for 2
      \*Acrylic crib blankets              7.80 for 2
      \*Receiving blankets                3.00 for 2
      \*See-through crib bumper (Creative)   9.00 ea.
      Washable acrylic blankets        5.00 ea.
      Bath towels                     2.50 ea.
      Facecloths (at least 3 per infant)    .75 ea.
      Vaseline (large jars)            1.00
      Desitin (large tube)             2.50
      Baby powder (large size)        1.00
      Pampers                      .50/child/day
                                      (approx.)

*Clothing*
      Undershirts (assorted sizes)      1.50 ea.
      \*Jumpsuits (assorted sizes)       3.00 ea.
      Sweaters (assorted sizes)        3.00 ea.
      Bibs, smocks                 .75 ea.
      Shirts                        2.00 ea.
      Corduroy pants (assorted sizes)    3.00 ea.
      Socks (assorted sizes)          1.00/3 pr.
      Mittens                    .50 ea.
      Hats                          1.00 ea.
      Scarves                   1.00 ea.

*Housekeeping*
      Plastic bags                 .75/box
      Covered diaper pails           3.00 ea.
      Mop                           3.00 ea.
      Broom                       1.50 ea.
      Sponges                 .50 ea.
      Cleaning supplies (soap, etc.)

---

\*For infants only.

## SAMPLE BUDGET FOR 16 INFANT-TODDLERS

|  | *High Cost* | *Low Cost* |
|---|---|---|
| **Staff** | | |
| Head teacher | $ 8,000 | $ 8,000 |
| Assistant teachers @ $6000/yr. | 18,000 | 12,000 |
| Volunteers ( 2 part-time) | | |
| Fringe benefits @ 10% | 2,600 | 2,000 |
| Administrative costs @ 5% | 1,300 | 1,000 |
| *Staff Subtotal* | $29,900 | $23,000 |
| | | |
| *Consultants* @ $50 x 12 mos. | $ 600 | |
| | | |
| **Equipment** | | |
| Educational | 2,000 | 400 and donated |
| Caretaking and housekeeping | 1,600 | 200 and donated |
| Office | 500 | Donated |
| Kitchen | 1,500 | Donated |
| Woodworking | 200 | Donated |
| *Equipment Subtotal* | $ 5,800 | $ 600 and donated |
| | | |
| **Supplies** | | |
| Educational | 200 | 50 and donated |
| Caretaking and housekeeping | 2,600 | 400 and donated |
| Office | 200 | Donated |
| *Supplies Subtotal* | $ 3,000 | $ 450 and donated |
| | | |
| **Food** | | |
| 60¢ x 16 children x 260 days | $ 2,496 | Donated |

|                                                                        | *High Cost* | *Low Cost* |
|------------------------------------------------------------------------|------------:|-----------:|
| *Space*                                                                |             |            |
| 710 sq. ft. (35 sq. ft./child = 560 sq. ft. plus 150 sq. ft. for kitchen and toilets) @ $2.50 per sq. ft. | $ 1,775 | Donated |
|                                                                        |             |            |
| *Utilities*                                                            |             |            |
| Telephone @ $15/month                                                  |         180 |        180 |
| Heat @ $12/month                                                       |         144 |        144 |
| Light @ $10/month                                                      |         120 |        120 |
| *Utilities Subtotal*                                                   |     $   444 |    $   444 |
|                                                                        |             |            |
| *Grand total*                                                          |    $44,015  |   $24,494  |

*PROGRESS REPORT*

Name of Child:

Teacher:

Classroom:

Date:

1. Physical Development:
   (Are there signs of illness and fatigue or of robust health and growth? Does the child seem to have a high or low energy level; etc.?)

2. Mental Development:
   (Child shows desire to explore and find out things; initiates and invents; uses language well for his level of development; etc.)

3. Social Development:
   (Response to teachers; making friends; learning to play with others; etc.)

4. Emotional Development:
   (Does the child show more joy or sadness, anger or amiability; what kinds of situations and behavior evoke strong emotions; etc.?)

5. Other:

## EVALUATION SHEET

### Head Teacher

Name _____

School _____

Class _____

Date _____

I.  Classroom Management:
    A.  Demonstrates a working knowledge of classroom environment which brings about responsible judgment involving decisions related to child care.

    B.  Shows creative imagination in providing a safe, warm, stimulating classroom environment for children.

    C.  Able to effectively and decisively cope with new and different problems.

    D.  Submits reports and keeps accurate records, forms, and observations.

II. Teaching Skills:
    A.  Displays the ability to perceive the group as a whole while demonstrating skill in working with small groups and individual children.

    B.  Exhibits thoughtful daily planning based on long-range goals and individual child needs.

    C.  Displays skill in planning, presenting, and maintaining materials and activities appropriate to the needs and interests of children in the classroom.

D.  Able to set and maintain limits for children so optimum learning can transpire.

III. Rapport:
  A.  Responds to children with warmth, friendliness, and humor.

  B.  Displays ability to relate to and work with not only children, but also other staff members and student teachers.

IV. Evaluation:
  A.  Able to recognize one's own successes and failures and the reasons for them.

  B.  Displays an active desire for learning, self-evaluation, and improvement.

## EVALUATION SHEET

### Assistant Teacher

Name _____

School_____

Class_____

Date _____

1. Demonstrates a working knowledge of classroom environment.

2. Demonstrates ability to initiate and sustain activities independent of head teacher.

3. Is responsible and consistent in maintaining limits established in the classrooms.

4. Recognizes individual and group needs and is organized to meet each successfully.

5. Able to effectively and decisively cope with new and different problems.

6. Responds to pupils with warmth, friendliness, and humor.

7. Displays ability to relate to and work with not only children but also other staff members and student teachers.

8. Able to recognize one's own successes and failures and the reasons for them.

9. Displays an active desire for learning, self-evaluation, and improvement.

## PRESCHOOL TEACHER-TRAINING PROGRAM GUIDES

Career Planning and Development of Nonprofessionals: Head Start Child Development Centers. Mimeographed draft. Washington, D.C.: prepared for Project Head Start (OEO) by Manpower Evaluation and Development Institute, 2430 Pennsylvania Ave., N.W., 1967. 168 pp.

Matthews, C., and Naylor, N. "Curriculum Development Program for Pre-School Teacher Aides—Quarterly Reports 1–5." 5 mimeographed reports. East St. Louis, Ill.: Delinquency Study and Youth Development Project, Southern Illinois University, November 1965–January 1967.

*New Careers: Generic Issues in the Human Services.* Washington, D.C.: prepared and published by National Institute for New Careers. University Research Corporation.

*New Careers: Procedural Guide for Program Development.* Washington, D.C.: information Clearing House New Careers Development Program, University Research Corporation.

Felsenfeld, N., et al. *New Careers in Social Service: The Training and Use of Subprofessionals in Child-Care Institutions.* Washington, D.C.: Institute for Youth Studies, Howard University, June 1967. 138 pp.

Fishman, J. R., et al. *Training for New Careers: The Community Apprentice Program,* pp. 29–34. Washington, D.C.: Institute for Youth Studies, Howard University.

## INSTITUTIONS OFFERING PROGRAMS IN CHILD CARE FOR PARAPROFESSIONALS

### Alabama

Tuskegee Institute, School of Education
Tuskegee, Ala. 36088
   Head Start Supplementary-Training Program
   Career Opportunities Program
   c/o Dr. Frankie G. Ellis (205) 727-8247

### Arizona

Arizona Western College
Yuma, Ariz. 85364
   c/o Virginia Smith, Child Care Aide

Central Arizona College
Coolidge, Ariz. 85228
   Teacher Assistant, Day Care-Operators
   Day Care-Attendants
   c/o Dale R. Gibson, Associate Dean
   Occupational Education

### California

American River College
Sacramento, Calif. 95841
   Early Childhood Education—Nursery School
   c/o Dr. Louis Quint, Asst. Dean
   Vocational Education (916) 484-8405

American River College
Sacramento, Calif. 95841
   The Nursery School
   c/o Mrs. Gene Dolan (916) 484-8433

Antelope Valley College
Lancaster, Calif. 93534
   Nursery School Aide
   c/o Mr. Jennings G. Brown
   (805) 943-3241 ext. 233

Bakersfield College
Bakersfield, Calif. 93305
   Teacher Aide, Nursery School Assistant
   c/o Mrs. Barbara Hoyt

City College of San Francisco
San Francisco, Calif. 94111
   Pre-Kindergarten Teacher Assistant
   c/o Mr. Jules Fraden (415) 587-7272

College of Marin
Kentfield, Calif. 94904
   Nursery School Teacher Aide
   c/o Mrs. Jean Ansley

College of the Canyons—Valencia
Valencia, Calif. 91355
   Early Childhood Education
   c/o Robert G. Pollock, Dean of Vocational-
   Technical Education (805) 259-7800, ext. 63

College of the Sequoias
Visalia, Calif. 93277
   Nursery School Teacher
   c/o Dr. Lincoln H. Hall (209) 732-4711

El Camino College
Torrance, Calif. 90506
   Early Childhood Teaching
   c/o Mr. Carl Meadows (213) 324-6631

Los Angeles Harbor College
Wilmington, Calif. 90744
   Special Education Aide, Nursery School Education
   c/o Mrs. Lenore Eisenstein (213) 835-0161

Merritt College
Oakland, Calif.
   Nursery School Assistant
   c/o Fred Ivey (415) 655-6110 ext. 94

Mount St. Mary's College
Los Angeles, Calif. 90049
   Child Care Worker
   c/o Miss Ruth Hoffman, Sister Mary Irene
   Flanagan (213) 272-8791

Napa College
Napa, Calif. 94558
Child Care Worker
c/o Mrs. Jen Terrace (707) 255-2100

Ohlone College
Fremont, Calif. 94537
Pre-School Assistant
c/o Mr. Robert Humason (415) 657-2100

Pacific Union College
Angwin, Calif. 94508
Nursery School Assistant (A.A.)
c/o Miss Esther Ambs, Chairman
Dept. of Home Economics (707) 965-6327

Palomar College
San Marcos, Calif. 92069
Pre-School Education

Riverside City College
Riverside, Calif. 92506
Nursery School Education
c/o Mrs. Louise Peterson (714) 684-3240

Sacramento City College
Sacramento, Calif. 95822
Nursery School Teachers
c/o Mrs. Bernice Clayton (916) 449-7431

San Bernardino Valley College
San Bernardino, Calif. 92403
Early Childhood Education
c/o Mr. F. Bruce Stewart (714) 885-0231
ext. 307

Southwestern College
Chula Vista, Calif. 92010
Nursery School Training/Teacher

University of California
Los Angeles, Calif.
Early Childhood/Technician
c/o Doris Sanson

Ventura College
Ventura, Calif. 93003
Early Childhood Education
c/o Charles C. Dahl (805) 642-3211, ext. 276

Victor Valley College
Victorville, Calif. 92392
Day Care, c/o Mrs. Pat Caldwell (714) 245-4271

*Connecticut*
Northwestern Connecticut Community College
Winsted, Conn. 06098
Child Care, c/o Robert Y. Allen

*Florida*
Santa Fe Junior College
Gainesville, Fla. 32601
Day Care Assistance
c/o Dr. Stanley Lynch (904) 378-5311
University of South Florida
Tampa, Fla. 33620
Supplementary Head Start Training Program
(Career Development)
c/o Dr. Michael Auleta (813) 974-2100

*Idaho*
Boise State College
Boise, Idaho 83707
Child Care Aides, c/o Dr. Gerald Wallace
and Dr. John Beitia (208) 385-1548

*Illinois*
College of Lake County
Grayslake, Ill. 60030
Child Care, c/o Mr. Fred Patterson
Danville Junior College
Danville, Ill. 61832
Early Childhood Services
c/o Mr. Robert Griggs
Elgin Community College
Elgin, Ill. 60120
Group Child Care
c/o Mrs. Paula Laubhan (312) 697-1000
Illinois Central College
East Peoria, Ill. 61611
Child Care, c/o Jean C. Aldag, Ph.D.

Kennedy-King College, Chicago City College
Chicago, Ill. 60621
  Teacher Aide, Residential Child Care
  Pre-School Education, Recreational Leadership
  c/o Dr. John Swift (312) 269-8000

Lincoln Land Community College
Springfield, Ill. 62703
  Child Care Technology
  c/o O. R. Vanderwater

Loop College, Chicago City College
Chicago, Ill. 60601
  Child Development Program
  Teacher Aide (Pre-School)
  c/o Mrs. June Aimen, Coordinator
  (312) 269-8089

Pestaloozi Froebel Teachers College
Chicago, Ill. 60601
  Nursery School Teaching
  c/o Mrs. A. L. Weston (312) 236-1671

Southeastern Illinois College
Harrisburg, Ill. 62946
  Child Care Aide
  c/o Mary Jo Oldham (618) 253-7655

Southern Illinois University
Edwardsville, Ill. 62025
  Child Care Services
  c/o Mr. Robert Rockwell, Coordinator
  (618) 692-2066

William Rainey Harper Community College
Palatine, Ill. 60067
  Child Care
  c/o Mr. Charles Joly (312) 359-4200


*Kansas*
  Donnelly College
  Kansas City, Kans. 66102
    Head Start Supplementary Training Program
    c/o Sister M. Richard Pendergast

University of Kansas
Lawrence, Kans. 66044
   Directors of Head Start Programs
   c/o Edward W. Scaggs, Director
   (913) 864-3352

*Kentucky*
   Eastern Kentucky University
   Richmond, Ky. 40475
   Child Care

*Maryland*
   Charles County Community College
   La Plata, Md. 20646
      Early Childhood Teacher Assoc.
      c/o Robert H. Turner (301) 934-2251

   Community College of Baltimore
   Baltimore, Md. 21215
      Early Childhood Education
      c/o Dr. Frederick S. Lee
      Director of General Studies
      (301) 462-5800, ext. 218

   Hagerstown Junior College
   Hagerstown, Md. 21740
      Early Childhood Teacher Aide

*Massachusetts*
   Aquinas Junior College
   Newton, Mass. 02158
      Early Childhood Education
      c/o Sister Philomene, CSJ 224-8134

   Bristol Community College
   Fall River, Mass. 02720
      Child Care Technology
      c/o Mr. Leonard Gaucher (617) 678-8211

   Fisher Junior College
   Boston, Mass. 02116
      Child Study Program
      c/o Dr. John F. Bowler (617) 536-4647

Garland Junior College
Boston, Mass. 02215
    Teacher Assistant and Teacher Aide Program
    c/o Mrs. Vera C. Weisz (617) 266-7585

Lesley College
Cambridge, Mass. 02138
    Dr. George L. Miller, V.P. for Academic Affairs
    & Dean of Teacher Education

Mass. Bay Community College
Watertown, Mass. 02172
    Career Degree Program in Early Child
    Assistant or Child Care (evening division)

Mount Ida Junior College
Newton Centre, Mass. 02159
    Child Study (Nursery School/Teacher Aide)
    c/o Mrs. Carol Storrs (617) 969-7000

Quinsigamond Community College
Worcester, Mass. 01606
    Early Childhood Assistant

Wheelock College
Boston, Mass.
    Early Childhood Education
    c/o Mrs. Fran Litman, Director
    Supplementary Training Program
    (617) 734-5200, ext. 303

*Michigan*
    University of Michigan
    Ann Arbor, Mich. 48104
        Day Care Mothers-in-service-training
        c/o Melinda Green (313) 763-0194

*Minnesota*
    Brainerd State Junior College
    Brainerd, Minn. 56401
        Child Development Teacher Assistant
        c/o Mrs. Virginia Almquist, Director
        (218) 829-4771

    University of Minnesota
    Minneapolis, Minn. 55455

Head Start Career Program
Early Childhood Development Program
c/o Professor Frank Wilderson
(612) 373-9880

*Missouri*

Penn Valley Community College
Kansas City, Miss. 64111
Day Care Aide, c/o Mrs. Geraldine Schermoly
(816) 561-8344

University of Missouri at K.C.
Kansas City, Miss. 64110
Children Worker, c/o Mr. Kenneth Kern

*Nebraska*

College of Saint Mary
Omaha, Nebr. 68124
Child Care and Development
c/o Sister Mary Mechtilde Hill, R.S.M.
(402) 393-8800

Creighton University
Omaha, Nebr. 68131
Child Care Technician, Aide, Assistant
c/o Mrs. Lou Guidira, Mr. John McGee

Peru State College
Peru, Nebr. 68421
Early Childhood Education
c/o Dr. Rex R. Shelly, Project Director
(402) 872-3815, ext. 87

*Nevada*

Elko Community College
Elko, Nev. 89801
Pre-Kindergarten Nursery School Program

*New Hampshire*

White Pines College
Chester, N.H. 03036
Child Care Assistant, c/o Mary Ann Pewers
Director of Admissions (603) 887-4401

*New Jersey*
    Essex County College
    Newark, N.J. 07102
        Early Childhood Educational Program
        c/o Dr. Ned Wilson (201) 621-2200, ext. 248

*New Mexico*
    New Mexico Highlands University
    Las Vegas, N.Mex. 87701
        Supplementary Training Program Headstart
        and Follow Through, Associate of Arts
        Degree in Early Childhood Education,
        c/o Mr. Cristobal D. Trujillo, Program Manager
        (505) 425-7511, ext. 384
    The College of Artesia
    Artesia, New Mexico 88210
        Head Start Workers
        c/o Mr. Loyal Clarke (505) 746-9862

*New York*
    A & T College, State University of New York
    Canton, N.Y. 13617
        Nursery Education, c/o Dr. Elizabeth Page
    Auburn Community College
    Auburn, N.Y. 13021
        Nursery Education—A.A.S.
        c/o Mr. Glen J. Snyder (315) 253-7549
    Broome Community College
    Binghamton, N.Y. 13902
        Nursery Education Aide
        c/o Carleton S. Everett, Dean of Continuing
        Education
    Cazenovia College
    Cazenovia, N.Y. 13035
        Child Study, c/o Mrs. Sheila Wall
        (315) 655-3466 ext. 234 or
        Mrs. Peg Taylor (315) 655-3466, ext. 232
    Dutchess Community College
    Poughkeepsie, N.Y. 12601
        Nursery Education, c/o Dr. Lawrence Monaco
        (914) 471-4500

Mater Dei College
Ogdensburg, N.Y. 13669
  Nursery Education Program
  c/o Sister M. Patricia (315) 393-5930

New School for Social Research
New York, N.Y. 10011
  Early Childhood Education Assistant
  c/o Dr. Sylvia Stuchin-Schwarts
  Human Relations Center (212) 293-1200

New York University
New York, N.Y.
  Teacher Aide (Early Childhood), c/o Dean
  Henry T. Lipman, NYU, Office of Community
  Services, One Fifth Ave., 4G, N.Y., N.Y.
  10003; Teacher Assistant, c/o Evelynne
  Patterson (212) 598-2148; Early Childhood
  Resource Specialist, c/o Dr. John Dill
  (212) 598-2203

Pace College-Westchester
Pleasantville, N.Y. 10570
  Aide, Day Care, c/o Dr. Edward B. Kenny,
  Project Manager (914) 769-3200, ext. 815

Rockland Community College
Suffern, N.Y. 10901
  Child Care Worker
  Mr. Leonard S. Romney (914) 356-4650, ext. 288

Staten Island Community College
Staten Island, N.Y. 10301
  Child Care Worker
  c/o Norma B. Chernok, Asst. Professor
  (212) 390-7563

Syracuse University
Syracuse, N.Y. 13210
  Preschool Teaching Aide
  c/o Dr. Ann Howe (315) 476-5541, ext. 2466

*North Carolina*
  Southeastern Community College
  Whiteville, N.C. 28472
    Child Care Worker, c/o Mr. William Ball

Southwestern Technical Institute
Sylva, N.C. 28779
> Child Care Worker, c/o Miss Lara Burchfield
> (704) 586-4091

*North Dakota*
University of North Dakota
Williston, N.Dak. 58801
> Head Start Tutoring
> c/o Mrs. Martha Huset (701) 572-6736

*Ohio*
Cuyahoga Community College
Cleveland, Ohio 44115
> Early Childhood Education
> c/o Dr. Fred Sutton

Lorain County Community College
Elyria, Ohio 44035
> Nursery School Assisting, c/o Emerson
> Lindamood (216) 365-4191

Muskigum Area Technical Institute
Gainesville, Ohio 43701
> Child Development Technology

Sinclair Community College
Dayton, Ohio 45402
> Early Childhood Education, Head Start and
> Follow Through, c/o Mrs. Mary Requarth,
> Supplementary Training Director
> (513) 224-0492

University of Cincinnati
Cincinnati, Ohio 45221
> Child Care Technology, c/o Dean Joseph
> J. Samuels (513) 475-2742

*Oklahoma*
Seminole Junior College
Seminole, Oklahoma 74868
> Child Development Technician
> c/o Jim Colclazier (405) 382-2589

*Oregon*
    Clackamas Community College
    Oregon City, Oregon 97045
        Child Care Education Specialist
        c/o Mrs. Patricia L. Lantz

*Pennsylvania*
    Bucks County Community College
    Swamp Road, Newton, Pa. 18940
        Early Childhood Education (Nursery School)
        c/o Dr. Ruth Frank (215) 968-4261, ext. 342
    Community College of Delaware County
    Media, Pa. 19063
        Nursery School Assistant
        c/o Mr. John Touhey (215) GL9-4800
        Dr. Virginia Harris (215) GL9-4800
    East Stroudsburg State College
    East Stroudsburg, Pa. 18301
        Day Care, Head Start
        c/o Dr. Florence McCormick
        (717) 421-4080 ext. 368
        Early Childhood Education Aide
        c/o Dr. Frank V. Kovacs
        (717) 421-4080 ext. 234
    Harrisburg Area Community College
    3300 Cameron Street Rd., Harrisburg, Pa. 17110
        Child & Day Care Program
        c/o Mr. John J. Ford
        236-9533, ext. 295
    Manor Junior College
    Jenkintown, Pa. 19046
        Assistant Teacher
        (Early Childhood Education-Nursery School)
        c/o Sister Emellia, Academic Dean
        (215) 885-2360
    Marywood College
    Scranton, Pa. 18509
        Head Start Supplementary Training
        Day Care Center
        c/o Sister M. Michel (717) 343-6521

Northampton County Area Community College
3835 Greenpond Road, Bethlehem, Pa. 18017
  Child Care Education (2 year associate
  degree program intended to train Head
  Start, nursery school, and day care
  center teachers and teacher aides),
  c/o Mrs. Constance Humes
  (215) 865-5351, ext. 66

Pennsylvania State University
University Park, Pa. 16802
  Paraprofessionals in Early Childhood
  Education (Harrisburg City Hospital)
  c/o Dr. Donald Peters (814) 865-1440

Temple University
Philadelphia, Pa. 19122
  Child Care Training Program
  c/o Mrs. Frances Vandivier
  (215) 787-8773

University of Pittsburgh, Greensburg Campus
122 N. Maple Ave., Greensburg, Pa. 15601
  Child Development Programs (first two years)
  c/o Carl F. Poke, Dean of Instruction

University of Pittsburgh, Titusville Campus
Titusville, Pa.
  Child Development and Child Care
  c/o Dr. Anne Pascasio (412) 683-1620, ext. 573

Villa Maria College
Erie, Pa. 16505
  Aids in Early Childhood Education
  c/o Sister M. Eunice Carlos (814) 838-1966,
  ext. 227

*Rhode Island*
  Roger Williams College
  Providence, R.I.
    Child Development and Teacher Training
    c/o Thomas M. Jones, Registrar

*South Carolina*
South Carolina State College
Orangeburg, S.C. 29115
Kindergarten Assistant, c/o Dr. Amelia S.
Roberts (803) 534-6560, ext. 235
University of South Carolina, Regional Campus
Columbia, S.C. 29208
Early Childhood, c/o Dr. John J. Duffy
(803) 777-4809
Two-year terminal associate degree program
in child development (graduates employable
as teacher aides and assistants)
c/o Mrs. Sue Martin, Coordinator,
College of General Studies (803) 777-8135

*South Dakota*
Presentation College
Aberdeen, S.Dak. 57401
Child Worker Technician,
c/o Sister M. Maurice Crowley, Chairman
Edu. Dept. 605-225-0420, ext. 341

*Tennessee*
Trevecca Nazarene College
Nashville, Tenn. 37210
Day Care Director-Teachers
c/o Dr. Wayne D. Lee

*Texas*
Eastfield College of the Dallas County Junior
College District
3737 Motley Drive, Mesquite, Tex. 75149
Child Development Assistant Program
(1 year certificate plan)
c/o Art Southerland, Associate Dean
Evening Administration
Our Lady of the Lake College
San Antonio, Tex. 78207
Institute in Early Childhood
c/o Mrs. Gerry Ahrendt (512) 434-6711,
ext. 238

San Antonio College
1300 San Pedro Avenue, San Antonio, Tex. 78212
    Child Day Care Associate
    c/o Mrs. Lucille Roch (512) 734-5381

Tarrant County Junior College District Northeast Campus
828 Harwood Rd., Hurst, Tex. 76053
    Child Development
    c/o Mrs. Peggy Solberg (817) 281-7860

Texas Woman's University, College of Household
Arts and Sciences
Box 24131, Denton, Tex. 76204
    Headstart Supplementary Training Program
    (for the state of Texas, except El Paso)
    c/o Dr. Jessie Bateman (817) 382-5441

University of Houston, College of Arts & Sciences
Houston, Tex. 77004
    Child Care, c/o Dr. Edward O. Bennett
    (213) 748-6600, ext. 271

University of Texas at El Paso
El Paso, Texas 79999
    Head-Start Supplemental Training Program
    c/o Dr. Joanna Armstrong, U.T.E.P., El Paso

*Vermont*
    Goddard College
    Plainfield, Vt. 05667
        Head Start and Day Care, c/o Mrs. Mary Jane Carlson
    Vermont College
    Montpelier, Vt. 05602
        Child Study

*Virginia*
    John Tyler Community College
    Chester, Va. 23831
        Instructional Aides in Early Childhood
        Education, c/o Mrs. Rosanne Hammes
        (703) 748-2221
    Lynchburg College
    Lynchburg, Va. 24504
        Head Start, c/o Dr. J. Edward Petty

*Washington*
    Bellevue Community College
    Bellevue, Wash. 98007
        Day Care Aide, Head Start Aide
        c/o Gloria Owens, Chairman (206) 641-2331
    Seattle University
    Seattle, Wash. 98122
        Head Start Supplementary Training
        c/o Dr. John Redmong
        (509) 613-0356

*West Virginia*
    West Virginia State College
    Institute, W.Va. 25112
        Kindergarten Aides
        c/o Dr. Harry V. Scott (304) 768-3981, ext. 304

*Wisconsin*
    Cardinal Stritch College
    Milwaukee, Wis. 53217
        Child Care Worker
        c/o Sister Jane Denning (414) 352-5400

*Wyoming*
    Eastern Wyoming College
    Torrington, Wyoming 82240
        Early Childhood Assistant, c/o Mr. Bill Marsh
        (307) 532-4191

## CASTLE SQUARE DAY CARE CENTER
## INFANT FEEDING PROGRAM

Mary-Brenda Cortell—Nutritionist

### Introduction

The world of an infant is a dependent one. Those of us responsible for feeding him have a unique opportunity to influence how he is to perceive that world.

If our aim is to provide a comfortable, warm, loving environment for him to grow and flourish in, then we must be aware of his physical and emotional as well as nutritional needs.

It is our belief that infants should be fed in a relaxed, pleasant atmosphere. They should be cared for by skilled people trained to recognize and respect their special needs—individuals who enjoy what they are doing.

Infants need to be picked up, held, and talked to while they are being fed. This kind of physical and oral contact gives babies a feeling that the world is a safe, reliable place; and helps to create a positive environment for the eating experience.

Of equal importance, of course, must be what he is fed. His meals need to be nutritionally well balanced. They should contain in kind and amount all the nutrients his body needs for healthful growth and body development.

The following handbook, I hope, will help in a practical way as a guide to meeting these needs.

### General Information for Infant Feeding

#### Formula Preparation

For precautionary health procedures, the presterilized prepared formula Similac with iron will be used. The formula should be placed into thoroughly washed bottles that have been put into the electric dishwasher with a 170° rinse.

Formula may give way to whole milk somewhere between three and four months or on physician's approval.

#### Solid Food

*Cereal.* Cereal may be added to diet at about five weeks.

*Preparation.* Start with rice cereal; dilute with prepared formula to the consistency most acceptable to baby.

*Amount.* Begin with one to two teaspoonfuls and work up to three to six tablespoons.

*Variety.* New cereals may be added one at a time at one week intervals. Hi-protein cereal is especially recommended for its greater nutritional value.

*Fruits.* Fruits are usually introduced at about two months. Fruits are good dessert foods; use simple fruits such as applesauce, bananas, peaches, or pears.

*Amount.* Begin with one to two teaspoonfuls and work up to three to six tablespoonfuls or ½ jar equivalent.

*Fruit Juices.* May be begun at second month; dilute two ounces of juice with two ounces of water; try simple juices such as apple, orange, pineapple, or grapefruit juice. This is a good morning or afternoon snack for a young baby.

*Meat.* Meats add protein and iron to the infant's diet. Meats may be begun at four months; begin with one to two teaspoonfuls and work up to three to six tablespoonfuls or ½ jar per meal. A jar of plain meat has much more protein and iron than a jar of a dinner.

Simple meats are preferred such as beef, lamb, turkey, chicken, pork, veal, or beef liver. If a baby does not seem to like the taste at first, begin slowly and mix with a little vegetable or fruit.

*Egg Yolk.* Egg yolk is a good source of iron—may be used once a day as soon as the physician allows.

*Vitamins.* The doctor will prescribe vitamins with fluoride; they should be given only in the amounts prescribed; too much can be as harmful as too little.

## SAMPLE MENU PLANS

*One to Two Months*
ON DEMAND    Not less than three- or more than five-hour intervals.

Breakfast    Formula, 4-6 ounces

| Snack | Formula, 4-6 ounces |
| Lunch | Formula, 4-6 ounces |
| Snack | Formula, 4-6 ounces |

### Two to Three Months

| Breakfast | Formula, 6-8 ounces<br>Cereal, diluted with formula, up to 6-8 tablespoonfuls |
| Snack | Juice, 2-4 ounces |
| Lunch | Formula, 6-8 ounces<br>Strained Vegetables, ¼-½ jar<br>Strained Fruit, ¼-½ jar |
| Snack | Juice, 2-4 ounces |
| Supper | Formula, 6-8 ounces<br>Cereal, up to 6-8 tablespoonfuls<br>Strained Fruit, ¼-½ jar |

### Three to Four Months

| Breakfast | Whole Milk, 6-8 ounces<br>Cereal, 6-8 tablespoonfuls |
| Snack | Juice, 2-4 ounces |
| Lunch | Milk, 6-8 ounces<br>Strained Vegetables, ¼-½ jar<br>Strained Fruit, ¼-½ jar |
| Snack | Juice, 2-4 ounces |
| Supper | Milk, 6-8 ounces<br>Cereal, 6-8 tablespoonfuls<br>Strained Fruit, ¼-½ jar |

### Four to Eight Months

| Breakfast | Cereal (baby cereal or other cereal high in iron)<br>Fruit, ½ jar |
| Lunch | Strained Meat, ½ jar<br>Strained Vegetables, ½ jar<br>Strained Fruit, ¼-½ jar |
| Snack | Vitamin C Juice, 4 ounces |

Supper                    Cereal or Meat and Vegetable
                          Fruit, ½ jar
                          Egg Yolk (as soon as recommended by
                          physician), ½ jar
24 ounces of Milk (3 bottles of 8 ounces or 4 bottles of six
ounces)

*Eight to Ten Months*
     Following the same pattern of menu as four to eight months,
          but the consistency may be changed to include junior
          foods rather than strained vegetables, fruit, and meat.
     From about ten months on, finger foods and soft table foods
          may be introduced—with the intent of weaning the
          child to table food somewhere between twelve to fif-
          teen months. Some suggestions are:
                    American cheese
                    Scrambled eggs
                    Vegetable soup
                    French toast
                    Tuna fish
                    Cooked vegetables
                    Small pieces of fresh fruit
                    Peanut butter
Infants may seem to demand less milk as their solid food
content increases. However, they should continue to be
offered 8 ounces of milk three times a day.

*Suggestions for Special Food Problems*

If a baby is *anemic*, his blood needs more iron:
     Baby cereal in boxes (or cream of wheat) is the best source
          of iron for babies.
     Liver is the meat highest in iron.
     Meat may be served one or two times a day and egg yolk
          once a day.

If a baby is *overweight:*
     He may not be hungry every time he cries; try not to over-
          feed.
     He may be just thirsty or want to be held.
     Avoid feeding him sweets, cookies, tonic, or chips.

Cut milk intake to 24 ounces.

Give baby lower-calorie foods instead of high-calorie foods
that have large amounts of fat or starches.

Low-calorie baby foods include:
    Plain fruit
    Plain meat
    Plain vegetables
    Plain egg yolk
    Skim milk

High-calorie foods include:
    Fruit dessert with tapioca
    Ham, chicken, or bacon
    Creamed vegetables
    Sweet and white potato
    Starchy dinners

If a baby has *diarrhea*, contact his physician.

In general, diminish the solid food intake as much as possible to allow the intestine to empty.

However, since a baby must not be allowed to get dehy-
drated, diluted skim milk may be given until the doctor is reached.

(This form must be filled out by a physician and returned to the day care center before school begins.)

## DAY CARE PROJECT
## DIVISION OF FAMILY HEALTH SERVICES
## MEDICAL RECORD

Child's Name _____

Parents' Name _____

Address _____

Doctor's Name & Address or Clinic Attended _____

_____

*Past History:*

    Birth Date _____

    Complications (if any) _____

    Allergies: _____

    Immunizations (date and reaction):

|  | Series Complete | Booster |
|---|---|---|
| Diphtheria |  |  |
| Whooping cough |  |  |
| Tetanus |  |  |
| Poliomyelitis |  |  |
| Smallpox |  |  |
| Measles |  |  |
| Other |  |  |

Acute Infections (specify date):

    Measles _____, Rubella _____, Chickenpox _____

    Mumps _____, Whooping cough _____

    Scarlet fever _____, Diphtheria _____

    Poliomyelitis _____, Other _____

Surgery:   Record in chronological order all surgical procedures, noting for each: the date, type of surgery, results, the surgeon, and the hospital at which it was performed.

_____

_____

_____

_____

_____

_____

_____

Injuries:   Record type, date, and sequelae of injuries.

_____

_____

_____

_____

Summary of admissions to hospitals:

_____

_____

_____

_____

Previously noted problems—please describe briefly.

Head:

Headaches _____, Eyes _____, Ears _____

Nose _____, Teeth _____, Throat _____

Respiratory System:

Cardiac System:

Gastrointestinal System:

Genitourinary System:

Neuromuscular System:

*Family History:*

T.B. _____, Rheumatism _____, Bright's Disease _____

Heart Trouble _____, Gout _____, Diabetes _____

Cancer _____, Nervousness or Insanity _____

Obesity _____, Asthma _____, Migraine _____

*Physical Examination:*

General Appearance: (Stature, gross deformities, etc.)

Height

Weight

Eyes and Vision

Ears and Hearing

Nose

Mouth and Teeth

Throat

Neck

Lymph Glands

Spine

Thorax

Lungs

Heart

Pulse

Abdomen

Genitalia

Extremities

Reflexes

Rectal

Summary of findings and recommendations:

_____

_____

_____

_____

_____

Physical exam recommended monthly? Every 3 months? Every 6 months? Once yearly?

Is there any physical disability that may interfere with the child's learning ability? Please describe.

_____

_____

_____

Date _____ Doctor's Signature _____

## PERMISSION SLIP: EMERGENCY MEDICAL CARE

In case of a medical emergency occurring while my child is attending the Castle Square Child Care Center, the following procedure will be carried out:

1. Contact Parent...................... Home Phone

   ...................... Business Phone

2. Contact Family Doctor............... Name

   ............... Phone Number

3. Arrange for emergency medical treatment.

I hereby authorize the Castle Square Day Care Center to follow the above procedure in arranging emergency medical treatment for my child:

———————————————————————————————

Parent's Signature: ————————————————————

Date: ————————————————

## EMERGENCY CARE PROCEDURE

1. When an acute illness or accident occurs at the day care center, teachers must notify the Supervisor who will call the child's parents and notify Beth Israel Hospital.

   A. Contact Parent........................Home Phone

      .....................Business Phone

   B. Contact Family Doctor.................Name

      .................Phone Number

   C. Arrange for emergency medical treatment.

2. A Xerox copy of each child's Emergency Medical Permission Slip must be taken on all field trips.

3. When an accident occurs on a field trip, teachers must call the Supervisor and bring the child to Beth Israel Hospital. The Supervisor will notify the child's parents and meet the teacher and child at Beth Israel Hospital, if necessary.

4. An accident report must be filled out and filed on the same day as the accident.

## ACCIDENT REPORT FORM

Child's Name: _____

Age: _____

Classroom: _____

Head teacher: _____

Date: _____

Time of accident: _____

Describe accident:

Treatment:

## SAMPLE LETTERS TO PARENTS

Dear Parents:

According to State Day Care Rules and Regulations, we are unable to accept at the Day Care Center any child with a diagnosed communicable disease (measles, mumps, chicken pox, etc.) or obvious acute illness. Therefore, please do not send your child to school when he is sick or has signs of possible contagious disease (new cold, sore throat, inflammation of the eyes, fever, rash, or diarrhea).

These medical precautions are taken for the protection of your child as well as the other children entrusted to our care. We thank you for your cooperation.

_____

Your child may have been exposed to chicken pox at the Day Care Center.

We wish to alert you to the symptoms of chicken pox and request that you keep your child home and notify us if he/she becomes ill. Initial symptoms include a slight fever and rash beginning on face or chest.

_____

Your child may have been exposed to German Measles at the Day Care Center.

We wish to alert you to the symptoms of German Measles and request that you keep your child home and notify us if he/she becomes ill. Initial symptoms consist of slight fever and signs of upper respiratory infections before the red rash begins.

If your child has not already had German Measles or been immunized, you may wish to have him immunized for German Measles by your doctor or health service.

Also, it is extremely important for any woman who is pregnant or suspects pregnancy, and may have come in contact with your child, to see a doctor or health service as soon as possible to check possible exposure to German Measles.

_____

Your child may have been exposed to measles at the Day Care Center.

We wish to alert you to the symptoms of measles and request that you keep your child home and notify us if he/she becomes ill. Initial symptoms consist of a fever and signs of upper respiratory infection including watery eyes, sore throat, and cough. On the second or third day bluish-white spots appear in the mouth and spotty red rash begins on the head and gradually spreads down the chest.

If your child has not already had measles or been immunized, you may wish to have him immunized for measles by your doctor or health service.

————————————————————

Your child may have been exposed to mumps at the Day Care Center.

We wish to alert you to the symptoms of mumps and request that you keep your child home and notify us if he/she becomes ill. Swelling of the glands begins behind the ears and spreads downward to the neck and lower jaws. A frequent addition to this is a scratchy throat and/or upper respiratory infection.

If your child has not already had mumps or been immunized, you may wish to have him immunized for mumps by your doctor or health service.

## APPLICATION FORM
## FAMILY HEALTH SERVICES—DAY CARE PROJECT

Castle Square Day Care Center
436 Tremont Street (Rear)
Boston, Massachusetts 02116

*Identifying Data:*

Date: _____

Name of Child: _____ Sex: _____
                Last     First     Middle

Age of Child: _____ Date of Birth: _____
                               Month    Day    Year

                 Place of Birth: _____
                                   City      State

*Family Data:*

Type of Family Unit (Circle One):     2 Parent     1 Parent

Father's Name (whether in the home or not): _____

      Address: _____Telephone #: _____

Mother's Name: _____

      Address: _____Telephone #: _____

Marital Status (Circle One):   Single      Married
                               Separated      Divorced

*Employment:*

Father or Guardian's Business Address: _____

      Name of Employer: _____

      Hours of Work: _____

Mother or Guardian's Business Address: _____

      Name of Employer: _____

      Hours of Work: _____

*Background Information:*

Father or Guardian's Age: _____

    Occupation: _____

    Place of Birth: _____

    Highest Level of Education Attained: _____

    Language(s) Spoken: _____

    Year of Arrival in the United States (if foreign born): ____

    Describe briefly the quality of Father's or Guardian's rela-

    tionship with your child: _____

    _____

Mother or Guardian's Age: _____

    Occupation: _____

    Place of Birth: _____

    Highest Level of Education Attained: _____

    Language(s) Spoken: _____

    Year of Arrival in the United States (if foreign born): ____

    Describe briefly the quality of Mother's or Guardian's re-

    lationship with your child: _____

    _____

Whom should we contact in case of Emergency?

    Name: _____Relationship: _____

    Address: _____Telephone #: _____

Name of your Doctor or Clinic: _____

    Address: _____

Please list other children in household:

    *First Name (Last, only if different) Age Name of School Grade*

    1. _____

    2. _____

    3. _____

    4. _____

    5. _____

Other Adults in Household:

Last Name     First Name     Relationship to Child

1. _____

2. _____

3. _____

How would you describe your child's role in your family? Is the child the "good little sister," "the black sheep," etc.: _____
_____

Please describe any alliances and frictions in the family that you think we should be aware of: _____
_____

Have there been any major changes in the family constellation such as divorce, or death? _____

Have there been any difficulties or crises in your family—such as, accidents, problems with the law, medical problems—that may have affected the emotional well-being of your child? _____
_____

*Child's Behavior Patterns and Habits:*

Please briefly describe an ordinary day in the life of your child, from his rising in the morning to going to bed:_____
_____
_____
_____

What is your child's favorite toy? _____Book? _____
Pet? _____Person? _____

Does your child have any particular habits or mannerisms, such as thumb-sucking, nail-biting? Please describe: _____
_____

Does your child have any particular fears, such as of dogs, or sirens; does he have nightmares? Please describe: _____

_____

Does your child use any peculiar words or expressions (such as "wee, wee," for urine) that may not be understood by an outsider? Please describe: _____

_____

In general, how does your child react to anxiety or a stressful situation? Does he cry, withdraw, throw tantrums: _____

_____

Has your child had any previous school or play-group experiences? Please describe: _____

_____

_____

Does your child relate well to other children? Does he seek friendships, or is he a loner? _____

_____

How does your child relate to adults? _____

_____

Has your child had the experience of being cared for by adults other than members of your family? Please describe: _____

_____

What is your accustomed mode of reassuring and rewarding your child? _____

_____

What is your accustomed mode of disciplining your child? What is your "philosophy" of discipline? _____

_____

Does your child speak English? _____Any other language? _____

Is he talkative, quiet, average? _____

To the best of your knowledge, does your child have any language problems, or learning disabilities? _____

Does your child have any emotional disturbances, or physical handicaps? _____

_____

How well do you anticipate your child will adjust to this day care program? _____

_____

Are there additional circumstances regarding your child's physical or emotional status that you would like us to be aware of?

_____

*Developmental History:*

Were there any birth difficulties? _____

_____

Does your child eat by himself? _____

Does your child enjoy eating? _____

If your child is on formula or baby food, please mention the type of diet and describe the pattern of eating in the course of one day: _____

_____

Is your child allergic to certain foods? _____If so, please list:

_____

How frequently does your child have between-meal snacks?

_____

Does your child have any allergies? _____

Do you have any particular concerns about your child's eating habits? _____

_____

Is your child toilet trained for urine? _____ for bowels?_____

If so, at approximately what age did your child become toilet trained for urine? _____ for bowels? _____

How frequently does he move his bowels? _____

How frequently do accidents occur? _____Do you have any particular concerns about your child's toilet habits? _____

Does your child sleep well? _____Does he usually nap? _____ How long? _____When? _____

Do you have any particular concerns about your child's sleeping habits? _____

_____

Is there anything else in your child's developmental history that you think we should be aware of? _____

If your child has any physical or emotional disability, would you please describe to the best of your ability the nature of that disability, its causation, prognosis, and treatment: _____

_____

Case Worker's Name _____Name of Welfare Office: _____Center's Address: _____

_____Telephone #: _____

## SUGGESTED MANIPULATIVE TOYS

| *Creative Playthings* | *Cost* |
|---|---|
| *Hanging balls | $3.50 |
| *Pulling sounds | 8.00 |
| *Turning balls | 7.00 |
| *Bell mobile | 8.00 |
| *Three wooden rattles | 5.00 |
| *Tube rattles | 2.50 |
| *Teething rings | 2.50 |
| *Teething jack | 2.00 |
| *Texture ball | 5.00 |
| *Clutch ball | 3.00 |
| *Small sponge ball | .50 ea. |
| *Grasshopper | 2.95 |
| *Anyway racer | 3.95 |
| *Pull balls | 4.00 |
| *Pull cubes | 4.00 |
| *Peg bus | 6.00 |
| *Boat train | 5.00 |
| *Pushing rods | 3.50 |
| *Hedgehogs | 2.00 |
| *Peg sandwich | 3.50 |
| Hammer balls | 5.00 |
| Hammer pegs | 5.00 |
| Floating animals | 4.50 |
| Bendable mirror | 4.00 |
| *Nesting and stacking | 5.00 |
| Plastic Puppets | 3.00 ea. |
| †Lock box | 14.00 |
| †Color lookers | 2.50 |

*Childcraft*

| | |
|---|---|
| *Cradle chimes | 3.50 |
| *Crib gym | 5.95 |
| *Gyro teether | 3.50 |
| *Octo teether | 1.50 |
| *See-hear-and-touch rattles | 5.50 |

| *Creative Playthings* | *Cost* |
|---|---|
| *Clutch ball | 1.95 |
| *Pattern pull | 2.75 |
| *Baby shapes | 2.50 |
| *Giant links | 1.95 |
| *Sound stack | 1.50 |
| *Finger exerciser | 1.50 |
| *Color stacking discs | 3.50 |
| *Nesting drums | 1.95 |
| *Learning Tower | 1.25 |
| Lacing shoe | 4.50 |
| Sequential sorting box | 7.95 |
| Play chips | 4.75 |
| Shape-sorting box | 5.00 |
| Kittie in the Kegs | 1.25 |
| Fit-a-Shape | 3.95 |
| Puzzle blocks | 2.00 |
| Pounding bench | 4.50 |
| Chunky Nuts | 2.50 |
| Workbench | 4.00 |
| Threading spools | 3.95 |
| Large beads and strings | 7.00 |
| Parquetry | 3.25 |
| Large peg board and pegs | 5.00 |
| Jumbo gear board | 5.95 |
| †Learning to Dress | 3.95 ea. |
| †*All by Himself; All by Herself* | 2.50 ea. |

---

*For infant-toddlers only.
†For toddler two-year-olds only.

## SUGGESTED WHEELED TOYS

|  | *Creative Playthings* | *Cost* |
|---|---|---|
| *Oversize Vehicles* | Riding tractor and trailer | $34.95 |
|  | Riding dump truck | 11.95 |
|  | Jumbo derrick truck | 14.95 |
|  | Giant Ride'em Bus | 26.95 |
|  | Riding truck | 30.95 |
|  | Four-wheel rider | 10.95 |
|  | Carriage | 27.95 |
| *Small-Wheeled Toys* | Blockomobiles | 9.95 |
|  | Garage | 11.95 |
|  | Marina | 11.95 |
|  | Wooden vehicles | 3.50 ea. |
|  | *Childcraft* |  |
| *Oversize Vehicles* | First wagon | 11.95 |
|  | Wee Wheeler | 7.95 |
|  | Tricycles (12″ front wheel) | 18.95 ea. |
|  | Wrecker | 13.95 |
|  | Freight van | 19.95 |
|  | Transfer truck | 16.50 |
|  | Delivery truck | 15.50 |
|  | Pickup truck | 10.95 |
|  | Dump truck | 13.50 |
|  | Sit-on freight train | 69.95 |
|  | Ferry boat | 8.95 |
|  | Steamer freight tanker | 9.95 |
|  | Bentwood carriage | 23.00 |
| *Small-Wheeled Vehicles* | Bulldozer | 8.95 |
|  | Jet airliner | 10.95 |
|  | Trailer dump truck | 10.50 |
|  | Fire engine | 8.95 |
|  | Transportation complex | 10.95 |
|  | Air shuttle | 3.00 |
|  | Helicopter | 2.50 |
|  | Highway fleet | 6.50 |
|  | Midi-Vehicle Set | 7.95 |

## SUGGESTED BLOCKS AND PROPS

| *Creative Playthings* | *Cost* |
|---|---|
| *Cloth bricks | $  7.95 |
| Cardboard blocks | 9.95 |
| Naef Spiel | 8.95 |
| Playplax | 8.95 |
| †Playroom block set | 57.95 |

| *Childcraft* | |
|---|---|
| †Nursery school set unit blocks | 105.00 |
| Apartment house | 32.95 |
| Big bedroom | 39.50 |
| Gas station | 17.50 |
| Block play traffic signs | 3.95 |
| Vinyl animals | 11.95 |
| Pliable people | 9.00 |

---

*For infants only.
†For two-year-olds only.

## SUGGESTED HOUSEKEEPING FURNISHINGS

| *Bedroom* | *High Cost* | *Low Cost* |
|---|---|---|
| Child-size bed | $ 14.00 | Homemade |
| Child-size cradle | 16.50 | Homemade |
| Child-size carriage | 25.00 | Homemade |
| Chest of drawers | 20.00 | Homemade (orange crates) |
| Rocking chair | 8.00 | Omit |
| White and black dolls, set of 4, $6 ea. | 24.00 | 24.00 |
| Easy-on doll clothes | Homemade | Homemade |
| Dress-up Clothes (Hats, pocketbooks, etc.) | Donated | Donated |
| Metal mirror | 16.00 | 16.00 |
| *Kitchen* | | |
| Kitchen set (refrigerator, stove, cupboard, sink) | 125.00 | Homemade |
| Tea set and chairs (2) | 40.00 | Homemade |
| Pots and pans | 6.00 | Donated |
| Tea service (cups, saucers, plates) | 9.00 | Homemade |
| Cutlery set (spoons, knives, forks) | 1.75 | Homemade |
| Housekeeping set (sweeper, duster, brooms, mops, dustpan) | 9.00 | Homemade |
| Doll high chair | 9.00 | Omit |
| Ironing board and wood iron | 16.00 | Omit |
| Plastic fruit set (lemon, orange, banana, apple, pear) | 4.00 | Omit |
| Plastic vegetable set (carrot, tomato, cucumber, pepper) | 4.00 | Omit |
| Empty cardboard containers (cereal boxes, salt, etc.) | Donated | Donated |
| Materials for doll clothes | 5.00 | 5.00 |
| Materials for construction | — | 25.00 |
| *Total* | $352.25 | $70.00 |

## SUGGESTED ART MATERIALS

| *Equipment* | *Cost* |
|---|---|
| Childcraft Interlox Wells | $ 4.95 |
| Flex-Flo dispenser | 3.75 |
| Easel brush ½" | 4.00 doz. |
| Teacher's shears | 2.10 |
| Desk stapler | 8.95 |
| Paper punch | .80 |

*Supplies*

*Paint*

| | |
|---|---|
| Primary tempera (quart) | 19.50 doz. |
| Finger paint (quart) | 17.50 doz. |
| Poster paint (quart) | 23.50 doz. |

*Paper*

| | |
|---|---|
| Newsprint (500 sheets) | 2.75 |
| Finger paint paper (100 sheets) | 25.00 doz. |
| Tissue paper (50 sheets) | 1.25 |
| Oak tag (50 sheets) | .95 |
| Construction paper, assorted colors (100 sheets) | .95 |
| Manila drawing paper (500) | 21.00 doz. |
| Brown wrapping paper | 9.20 |

*Miscellaneous*

| | |
|---|---|
| Elmer's Glue | 4.85 |
| Felt-tip markers, assorted colors | 3.95 set |
| Oversized hexagonal wax crayons, assorted colors | .50 set |
| Cray-Pas, assorted colors | .50 set |
| Play-Doh, assorted colors | 1.50 |
| Popsicle sticks (1000) | 2.25 |
| Pipe cleaners, assorted colors (100) | 1.25 |
| Assorted materials for collage | Donated |

## SUGGESTED TABLE TOYS

| *Creative Playthings* | *Cost* |
|---|---|
| Things puzzles | $ 4.00 |
| Number sorter | 4.00 |
| Wooden puzzles | 4.00 |
| Circles, squares, and triangles | 5.00 |
| Shape dominoes | 4.00 |
| †Look-in puzzles | 6.00 ea. |
| Design cubes | 6.00 |
| †Magnetic shapes | 4.00 |
| †Number pairs | 3.50 |
| †Lottos | 3.95 |
| †Colors and Shapes | 9.95 |
| †Small magnets | 1.95 |
| Table-top blocks | 10.95 |
| *Childcraft* | |
| See-into Puzzles | 3.00 ea. |
| Puzzles with small knobs | 3.00 ea. |
| Beginner's wood inlay puzzles | 2.00 ea. |
| Peg-sorting board | 4.75 |
| Vehicle puzzle | 3.00 |
| Zoo puzzle | 2.75 |
| Puzzles with small knobs | 3.00 ea. |
| Knob puzzles | 6.25 ea. |
| Simply cut puzzles | 2.00 ea. |
| Beginner's Community Scene Puzzles | 2.00 ea. |
| First jigsaws | 1.50 ea. |
| Stand-up Puzzles | 2.00 ea. |
| Play Rings | 4.00 |
| Structural blocks | 11.95 |
| Decreasing Ingets | 1.95 ea. |
| †Tactile letter blocks | 22.95 set |
| Number Learner | 1.95 |
| Tactile domino blocks | 9.95 |
| Beaded abacus | 4.00 |
| †Rods and counters | 5.50 |
| †Add-a-Count scale | 6.50 |
| †Pan Balance scale | 9.95 |
| †Tactile time teacher | 4.95 |

†For toddler two-year-olds only.

## SUGGESTED BOOKS FOR INFANT-TODDLERS

| Aldis, Dorothy | *All Together* | Putnam | 1952 |
|---|---|---|---|
| Allen, Marie | *A Pocketful of Poems* | Harper | 1957 |
| | *Baby's ABC* | Platt & Munk | |
| | *Baby's First Book* | Platt & Munk | |
| | *Baby's Playthings* | Platt & Munk | |
| | *Baby's Things* | Platt & Munk | |
| Brown, Margaret Wise | *A Child's Goodnight Book* | Young Scott Books | 1950 |
| Brown, Margaret | *Baby Animals* | Golden | |
| | *Goodnight Moon* | Harper | 1947 |
| | *The Noisy Book* | Scott | 1939 |
| Davis, Daphne | *The Baby Animal Book* | Golden | 1964 |
| Ets, Marie Hall | *Gilberto and the Wind* | Viking | 1963 |
| Flack, Marjorie | *Ask Mr. Bear* | Macmillan | 1932 |
| | *Angus and the Ducks* | Doubleday | 1930 |
| | *Angus and the Cat* | Doubleday | 1931 |
| Frank, Josette | *Poems to Read to the Very Young* | Random | 1961 |
| | *More Poems to Read to the Very Young* | Random | 1967 |
| Geismer, Barbara | *Very Young Verse* | Houghton | |
| Krugllovsky, P. | *The Very Little Boy* | Doubleday | 1962 |
| | *The Very Little Girl* | Doubleday | 1962 |
| Krauss, Ruth | *The Bundle Book* | Harper | 1951 |
| Langstaff, N. | *A Tiny Baby for You* | Harcourt | 1955 |
| | *My First Toys* | Platt & Munk | |
| Pfloog, Jan | *The Farm Book* | Golden | 1964 |
| Petersham, Maud & Miska | *The Box With Red Wheels* | Macmillan | 1949 |
| Steiner, Charlotte | *My Slippers Are Red* | Knopf | 1957 |
| | *Things to See* | Platt & Munk | |
| Wright, Blanche, ed. | *The Real Mother Goose* | Rand McNally | 1966 |

## SUGGESTED BOOKS FOR TODDLER TWO-YEAR-OLDS

| | | | |
|---|---|---|---|
| Anglund, Joan | *A Friend Is Someone Who Likes You* | Harcourt | 1958 |
| Bright, Robert | *My Red Umbrella* | Morrow | 1959 |
| Brown, Margaret W. | *The Diggers* | Harper | 1960 |
| | *The Golden Bunny* | Golden | |
| | *The Runaway Bunny* | Harper | 1942 |
| | *Sleepy Little Lion* | Golden | |
| Brown, Myra | *My Daddy's Visiting Our School Today* | Watts | 1961 |
| Buckley, Helen | *Grandfather and I* | Lothrop | 1959 |
| | *Grandmother and I* | Lothrop | 1961 |
| | *Josie and the Snow* | Lothrop | 1964 |
| | *The Little Boy and the Birthdays* | Lothrop | 1965 |
| | *My Sister and I* | Lothrop | 1963 |
| | *Too Many Crackers* | Lothrop | 1966 |
| Burton, Virginia | *Katy and the Big Snow* | Houghton | 1943 |
| Cohen, Miriam | *Will I Have a Friend?* | Macmillan | 1967 |
| Deforest, Charlotte | *The Prancing Pony Nursery Rhymes From Japan* | Weatherhill | 1967 |
| Ets, Marie Hall | *Another Day* | Viking | 1953 |
| | *In the Forest* | Viking | 1944 |
| | *Just Me* | Viking | 1965 |
| | *Play With Me* | Viking | 1955 |
| Exler, Samuel | *Growing and Changing* | Lothrop | 1957 |
| Flack, Marjorie | *Story About Ping* | Viking | 1933 |
| Freeman, Don | *Corduroy* | Viking | 1968 |
| Green, Mary M. | *Everybody Eats* | Scott | 1940 |
| | *Everybody Has a House* | Scott | 1944 |
| | *Is It Hard? Is It Easy?* | Young Scott | 1960 |

| | | | |
|---|---|---|---|
| Hader, Berta & Elmer | *The Big Snow* | Macmillan | 1948 |
| Hastings, Eveline | *Pearl Goes to School* | Follett | 1962 |
| Hoban, Russell | *A Baby Sister for Frances* | Harper | 1964 |
| | *Bed Time for Frances* | Harper | 1960 |
| | *A Birthday for Frances* | Harper | 1968 |
| Kay, Helen | *One Mitten Lewis* | Lothrop | 1955 |
| Keats, Ezra Jack | *Peter's Chair* | Harper | 1967 |
| | *Snowy Day* | Viking | 1962 |
| | *Whistle for Willie* | Viking | 1964 |
| Kepes, Juliet | *Frogs Merry* | Pantheon | 1961 |
| Kessler, Ethel | *Do Baby Bears Sit on Chairs?* | Doubleday | 1961 |
| Kessler, Ethel & Leonard | *The Big Red Bus* | Doubleday | 1957 |
| | *The Day Daddy Stayed Home* | Doubleday | 1957 |
| | *Kim and Me* | Doubleday | 1960 |
| Knight, Hilary | *Where's Wallace?* | Harper | 1964 |
| Krasilovsky, Phyllis | *Scaredy Cat* | Macmillan | 1959 |
| Krauss, Ruth | *Bears* | Harper | 1948 |
| | *The Backward Day* | Harper | 1956 |
| Krauss, Ruth | *The Growing Story* | Harper | 1947 |
| Langstaff, John | *Over in the Meadow* | Harcourt | 1957 |
| Leaf, Munro | *The Story of Ferdinand* | Viking | 1936 |
| Lenski, Louis | *Papa Small* | Oxford | 1951 |
| Lewis, Richard | *In a Spring Garden* | Dial | 1965 |
| Lowrey, Janette | *The Poky Little Puppy* | Golden | 1942 |
| Marino, Dorothy | *Goodbye Thunderstorm* | Lippincott | 1958 |
| | *Where Are the Mothers?* | Lippincott | 1959 |

| | | | |
|---|---|---|---|
| McCloskey, Robert | *Blueberries for Sal* | Viking | 1948 |
| | *Make Way for Ducklings* | Viking | 1941 |
| Miles, Betty | *Having a Friend* | Knopf | 1959 |
| Milne, A. A. | *When We Were Very Young* | Dutton | 1924 |
| Minarik, Else | *Little Bear* | Harper | 1957 |
| Moncure, Jane | *Pinney's Day at Play School* | Lothrop | 1955 |
| Munari, Bruno | *Bruno Munari's Zoo* | World | 1963 |
| O'Neill, Mary | *Hailstones & Halibut Bones* | Doubleday | 1961 |
| Oxenbury, Helen | *Numbers of Things* | Watts | 1968 |
| Parish, Peggy | *Hush, Hush, It's Sleepy Time* | Golden | 1968 |
| Piper, Watty | *The Little Engine That Could* | Platt & Munk | 1930 |
| Potter, Beatrix | *The Tale of Peter Rabbit* | Warne | 1902 |
| Provenson, A. & M. | *What Is Color?* | Golden | 1967 |
| Puner, Helen | *Daddies: What They Do All Day* | Lothrop | 1946 |
| Rey, H. A. | *Curious George* | Houghton | 1946 |
| Rey, Margaret and H. A. | *Curious George Goes to the Hospital* | Houghton | 1966 |
| Schatz, Letta | *Whiskers My Cat* | McGraw | 1967 |
| Schlein, Miriam | *Heavy Is a Hippopotamus* | Scott | 1954 |
| Schwartz, Julius | *I Know a Magic House* | McGraw | 1956 |
| Scott, Ann | *Big Cowboy Western* | Lothrop | 1965 |
| | *Sam* | McGraw | 1967 |
| Selsam, Millicent | *Seeds and More Seeds* | Harper | 1959 |
| Simon, Norma | *What Do I Say?* | Whitman | 1967 |
| Skaar, Grace | *All About Dogs* | Young Scott | 1966 |
| | *What Do the Animals Say?* | Young Scott | 1968 |

| | | | |
|---|---|---|---|
| Slobodkina,<br>  Esphyr | *Caps for Sale* | Young Scott | 1947 |
| Stevenson, R. L. | *A Child's Garden of*<br>  *Verses* ∙ | Penguin | 1952 |
| Seuss, Dr.<br>  (Geisel,<br>  Theo.) | *And to Think I Saw*<br>  *It on Mulberry*<br>  *Street* | Vanguard | 1937 |
| | *The Cat in the Hat* | Random | 1957 |
| Thompson,<br>  Blanche | *All the Silver*<br>  *Pennies* | Macmillan | 1967 |
| Thompson, Jean | *Poems to Grow On* | Beacon | 1957 |
| Tressett, Alvin | *Hide and Seek Fog* | Lothrop | 1965 |
| | *Hi Mister Robin!* | Lothrop | 1950 |
| | *Rain Drop Splash* | Lothrop | 1946 |
| | *Wake Up Farm* | Lothrop | 1955 |
| Tudor, Tasha | *Around the Year* | Walck | |
| Udry, Janice | *A Tree Is Nice* | Harper | 1956 |
| Wildsmith, Brian | *Brian Wildsmith's*<br>  *ABC* | Watts | 1963 |
| Wright, Ethel | *Saturday Walk* | Scott | 1954 |
| Yashima, Taro | *Umbrella* | Viking | 1958 |
| | *Youngest One* | Viking | 1962 |
| Ziner, Feenie | *Counting Carnival* | Coward-<br>          McCann | 1962 |
| Zion, Gene | *Harry the Dirty Dog* | Harper | 1956 |
| | *No Roses for Harry* | Harper | 1957 |
| Zolotow,<br>  Charlotte | *The Storm Book* | Harper | 1952 |

## SUGGESTED MUSICAL INSTRUMENTS

| *Creative Playthings* | *Cost* |
|---|---|
| Drum | $ 6.00 |
| Rhythm band set | 10.95 |

| *Childcraft* | |
|---|---|
| Rhythm band primary set | 15.00 |
| Jingle bells | .75 |
| Hohner wrist bells | .90 |
| Maracas | 1.95 |
| Hohner tambourines | 5.00 |
| Mini-drums | 3.00 |
| Av-to-Harp | 42.50 |
| Xylophone | 3.50 |
| Portable phonograph | 75.00 |

## SUGGESTED RECORDS

| | |
|---|---|
| *Adventures in Rhythm* | $4.15 |
| *American Folk Songs for Little Ones* | 5.95 |
| *American Games and Activity Songs for Children* | 5.95 |
| *American Play Parties* | 5.95 |
| *Birds, Beasts, Bugs and Little Fish* | 5.95 |
| *Burl Ives Sings Little White Duck* | 1.89 |
| *Rhythm and Game Songs for Little Ones* | 5.95 |
| *Song and Play-Time* | 5.95 |
| *Songs to Grow On—Nursery Days* | 4.15 |
| *You'll Sing a Song and I'll Sing a Song* | 5.95 |

Aaron, David, and Bonnie P. Winawer. *Child's Play: A Creative Approach to Play Spaces for Today's Children.* New York: Harper & Row, 1968.

Abramson, P. *Schools for Early Childhood: Profiles of Significant Schools.* New York: Educational Facilities Laboratories, 477 Madison Ave., 1970.

> Hilltop and KLH in Boston, a commercial center, the New Nursery School, Glen Nimnicht's toy library, and others.

Adams, Bert N. *The American Family.* Chicago: Markham Publishing Co., 1971.

Allen, Marjorie. *Planning for Play.* Cambridge: M.I.T. Press, 1969.

Alschler, Rose H. *Children's Centers.* New York: William Morrow Co., 1942.

Ambrose, A. *Stimulation in Early Infancy.* New York: Academic Press, 1969.

> Report of an international conference.

Andrews, Gladys. *Creative Rhythmic Movement for Children.* New York: Prentice-Hall, Inc., 1954.

Arbuthnot, May Hill. *Children and Books.* Chicago: Scott, Foresman and Co., 1957.

Architectural Research Laboratory. *An Annotated Bibliography on Early Childhood.* Ann Arbor: University of Michigan Publications Distribution Service, 1970.

Aries, P. *Centuries of Childhood: A Social History of Family Life.* New York: Vintage, 1962. (Originally published in French, 1960.)

Baldwin, Alfred. *Theories of Child Development.* New York: John Wiley & Sons, Inc., 1968.

Beadle, Muriel. *A Child's Mind.* New York: Doubleday & Co., 1971.

Bell, Robert R. *Premarital Sex in a Changing Society.* New Jersey: Prentice-Hall, Inc., 1966.

Bettelheim, Bruno. *The Children of the Dream: Communal Child-Rearing and American Education.* New York: Macmillan Co., 1969.

Bland, Jane Cooper. *Art of the Young Child.* New York: The Museum of Modern Art, 1958.

Brazelton, T. Berry. *Infants and Mothers.* New York: Dell Publishing Co., 1969.

Brearly, Molly, and Elizabeth Hitchfield. *A Teacher's Guide to Reading Piaget.* London: Routledge and Kegan Paul, 1966.

Brearly, Molly, ed. *The Teaching of Young Children—Some Applications of Piaget's Theory.* New York: Schocken Books, 1970.

Breckenridge, Marian, and Margaret Nesbitt. *Growth and Development of the Young Child.* Philadelphia: W. B. Saunders, 1963.

Bronfenbrenner, U. *Two Worlds of Childhood: U.S. and U.S.S.R.* New York: Russell Sage Foundation, 1970.

Bruner, Jerome S. *Processes of Cognitive Growth: Infancy.* Worcester: Clark University Press with Barre Publishers, 1968.

Caldwell, Bettye M. "Programmed Day Care for the Very Young Child—A Preliminary Report," *Journal of Marriage and the Family,* 26: 481–488.

————. "What is the Optimal Learning Environment for the Young Child?," *American Journal of Orthopsychiatry,* 37, No. 1 (1961), pp. 18–21.

Canner, Norma . . . *and a time to dance.* Boston: Beacon Press, 1968.

Chauncy, H. *Soviet Preschool Education, Vol. I: Program of Instruction; Vol. II: Teachers Commentary.* New York: Holt, Rinehart and Winston, 1969.

*Childhood in Contemporary Cultures.* Edited by Margaret Mead and Martha Wolfenstein. Chicago: University of Chicago Press, 1955.

Cohen, Dorothy H. and Virginia Stern. *Observing and Recording the Behavior of Young Children.* New York: Teachers College Press, Columbia University, 1969.

Cole, Natalie R. *Children's Art From Deep Down Inside.* New York: The John Day Co., 1966.

————. *The Arts in the Classroom.* New York: The John Day Co., 1940.

Dawson, Mildred A., and Frieda H. Dingee. *Children Learn the Language Arts.* Minneapolis: Burgess Publishing Co., 1959.

Dinkmeyer, Don, and Rudolph Dreikurs. *Encouraging Children to Learn: The Encouragement Process.* Englewood Cliffs, N.J.: Prentice-Hall, Inc., 1963.

Dittmann, L. L., ed. *Early Child Care: The New Perspectives.* New York: Atherton, 1968.
    Excellent articles about the past 60 years, here and abroad: Caldwell & Richmond; H. Robinson.

Elkind, D. "Giant in the Nursery—Jean Piaget," *Contemporary Readings in Psychology* by J. Foley, R. Lockhart, and D. Messick. New York: Harper & Row, 1970.

Erikson, Erik. *Childhood and Society.* New York: W. W. Norton & Co., 1963.

Evans, E. Belle, Beth Shub, and Marlene Weinstein. *Day Care.* Boston: Beacon Press, 1971.

Fitzpatrick, Elsie, Nicholas Eastmen, and Sharon Reeder. *Maternity Nursing.* Philadelphia: J. B. Lippincott Co., 1966.

Flanagan, Geraldine. *The First Nine Months of Life.* New York: Pocket Books, 1966.

Flavell, J. *The Developmental Psychology of Jean Piaget.* Princeton, New Jersey: Van Nostrand Co., 1963.

Frost, Joe L., ed. *Early Childhood Education Rediscovered.* New York: Holt, Rinehart and Winston, Inc., 1968.

Gaitskell, Charles and Al Hurwitz. *Children and Their Art.* New York: Harcourt, Brace & World, 1970.

Gardner, D. Bruce. *Development in Early Childhood: The Preschool Years.* New York: Harper & Row, 1964.

Gesell, Arnold, et al. *The First Five Years of Life.* New York: Harper & Row, 1940.

Gesell, Arnold, and Catherine Amatruda. *Developmental Diagnosis.* New York: Harper & Row, 1964.

Gordon, Ira J. *Baby Learning Through Baby Play.* New York: St. Martins Press, 1970.

Gordon, I. J., and J. R. Lally. *Intellectual Stimulation for Infants and Toddlers.* Gainesville, Florida: Institute for the Development of Human Resources, University of Florida, 1967.

Haith, M. M. "Day Care and Intervention Programs for Infants Under Two Years of Age." Mimeographed. Cambridge, Mass.: Harvard University, 1970.
    The best review of infant programs.

Hammond, Sarah Lou, Rule Dales, and Dora Skipper. *Good Schools for Young Children*. New York: The Macmillan Co., 1963.

Hawkins, D. F., J. R. Curran, and J. W. Jordan. *Industry Related Day Care: the KLH Child Development Center, Part I*. Needham, Mass.: Social Administration Research Institute, n.d.
    An evaluation by Harvard Business School faculty.

Hechinger, Fred M., ed. *Pre-School Education Today*. Garden City, New York: Doubleday & Co., 1966.

Hoffman, Martin L., and Lois W. *Review of Child Development Research*, Volume 1. New York: Russell Sage Foundation, 1964.

————. *Review of Child Development Research*, Volume 2. New York: Russell Sage Foundation, 1966.

Hymes, James L. *A Child Development Point of View*. Englewood Cliffs, N.J.: Prentice-Hall, 1955.

————. *The Child Under Six*. Englewood Cliffs, N.J.: Prentice-Hall, 1963.

Isaacs, S. *The Nursery Years: the Mind of the Child from Birth to Six*. New York: Vanguard.

————. *Intellectual Growth in Young Children*. New York: Schocken, 1966.

Jefferson, Blanche. *Teaching Art to Children*. Boston: Allyn and Bacon, 1963.

Kami, Constance, and Norma L. Radin. "A Framework for a Pre-School Curriculum Based on Piaget's Theory." Ypsilanti, Michigan, Public Schools.

Landreth, Catherine. *The Psychology of Early Childhood*. New York: Alfred Knopf, 1958.

Lederman, Alfred, and Alfred Trachecl. *Creative Playgrounds and Recreation Centers*. New York: Frederick A. Praeger, Inc., 1967.

Leeper, Sarah, et al. *Good Schools for Young Children: A Guide for Working with 3, 4 and 5 Year Olds*. New York: The Macmillan Co., 1968.

Leonard, George B. *Education and Ecstasy*. New York: A Delta Book, 1968.

Lindstrom, Miriam. *Children's Art*. Berkeley, California: University of California Press, 1969.

Litman, F. "Teacher Aides: Relationships Between Teachers and Paraprofessionals," *As the Twig Is Bent.* Edited by R. Anderson and H. Shane. Boston: Houghton Mifflin, in press.

Lowenfield, Victor. *Your Child and His Art.* New York: The Macmillan Co., 1954.

Maccoby, E. E. "Effects of the Mass Media," *Review of Child Development Research,* Vol. 1. Edited by M. L. Hoffman and L. W. Hoffman. New York: Russell Sage Foundation, 1964, pp. 323–348.

Maier, Henry W. *Three Theories of Child Development.* New York: Harper & Row, 1965.

Matterson, E. M. *Play and Playthings for the Pre-School Child.* Baltimore: Penguin Books, 1967.

Murphy, Lois Barclay. *The Widening World of Childhood.* New York: Basic Books, 1962.

Mussen, Paul, John Conger, and Jerome Kagen. *Child Development and Personality.* New York: Harper & Row, 1963.

Phillips, John L. *The Origins of Intellect: Piaget's Theory.* San Francisco: W. H. Freeman and Co., 1969.

Piaget, Jean. *The Origins of Intelligence in Children.* Trans. by Margaret Cook. New York: W. W. Norton, 1952.

Pines, Maya. *Revolution in Learning: The Years From Birth to Six.* New York: Harper & Row, 1966.

Pitcher, E. G., Lasher, Feinberg, Hammond, et al. *Helping Young Children Learn.* Columbus, Ohio: Merrill Co., 1966.

Provence, Sally, and R. Lipton. *Infants in Institutions.* New York: International Universities Press, 1962.

Rudeman, Florence. *Child Care and Working Mothers.* New York: Child Welfare League of America, Inc., 1960.

Russell, David H. *Children's Thinking.* New York: Blaisdell Publishing Company, 1965.

Schneider, Earl, ed. *The Pet Library.* New York: 1969.

Sears, Robert. *Identification and Child Rearing.* Stanford, Calif.: Stanford University Press, 1965.

Sheehy, Emma. *Children Discover Music and Dance.* New York: Henry Holt, 1959.

———. *There's Music in Children.* New York: Henry Holt, 1946.

Sigel, Irvin, and Frank H. Hooper, eds. *Logical Thinking in Children: Research Based on Piaget's Theory.* New York: Holt, Rinehart and Winston, Inc., 1968.

Stendler, D., ed. *Readings in Child Behavior and Development.* New York: Harcourt, Brace & World, 1964.

Stone, L. Joseph, and Joseph Church. *Childhood and Adolescence.* New York: Random House, 1968.

Taylor, Harold. *Art and the Intellect.* Garden City, New York: distributed by Doubleday and Company for Museum of Modern Art, 1960.

Van der Eyken, W. *The Pre-School Years.* Middlesex, England: Penguin Books, 1967.

Vygotsky, L. S. *Thought and Language.* Cambridge, Mass.: M.I.T. Press, 1966.

Wann, K. D., M. Dorn, and E. A. Liddle. *Fostering Intellectual Development in Young Children.* New York: Teachers College Press, 1962.

One of the first books with more cognitive emphasis.

# INDEX

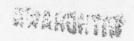